托业桥考试全攻略

[美] 罗纳德·赖利（Renald Rilcy）编著

蒋璀玢 译

中国人民大学出版社

·北 京·

目　录

第1章

考试介绍

1.1　何为“托业桥”考试

这一考试是由教育评估领域的世界领导者美国教育考试服务中心ETS（Educational Testing Service）于 2001 年发起的。众所周知的TOEIC（托业）和TOEFL（托福）考试也是由ETS研发的。

托业桥测试用于评估母语为非英语人士在日常生活中以及国际化的办工场所内使用英语交流的能力。托业桥的测评范围是在英语初学者至中低水平之间（类似于 CEF 考试中 A1~B1 水平）。

托业桥测试完全符合ETS对于质量与公正的标准要求，确保是值得高度信赖的英语水平评估工具。

1.2　托业桥考试的目的

托业桥考试是一种测试英语熟练程度的客观方法，适用于各种类型的英语初学者及中低水平者，包括：

—中学、大专院校学生

—国际化办公场所的学习者

同时在如下机构/个人方面，托业桥也可以作为决策工具使用：

私立与公立的语言培训机构

—将英语水平相当的学生进行分组

—鼓励学生向设定目标努力

—通过外部的、可信赖的证书保证培训计划的有效性

高等教育机构

—通过设定特殊课程目标提高主动学习性

—检查学生在课程中不同阶段的进展状况

—在学生个人简历中，提供语言熟练程度的准确信息

公司企业

—识别员工是否需要更进一步的语言培训

—设置精准的学习目标及分配培训的预算
—语言测评时可以精确地比较英语掌握水平
—给予语言交流能力强者以奖励

个人申请者

—愿意持有一张可以证明其英语水平的国际认可的证书的研究生
—求职者

1.3　托业桥考试的结构

托业桥考试是纸笔测试，由 100 道多项选择题组成，分为两部分：**听力理解**和**阅读理解**。

该测试需要一个小时完成。但是，应试者还需要留出额外的 30 分钟来完成管理流程，填写教育背景、工作经历及英语经验的小问卷。关于上述这些问题的反馈信息将严格保密，并对测试分数没有影响。这些是用于帮助 ETS 收集数据来分析影响测试成绩和提高英语水平的因素。

参加托业桥考试的应试者会得到一本试题册和一张单独的答题卡。所有的问题均需用铅笔在答题卡的(A)，(B)，(C)，(D)中勾选出答案。

每一部分都有具体的答题说明。

听力理解部分

听力理解部分大约用时 25 分钟，题号从 1~50，分为三个 PART：

PART	题型	题目数量
1	图片题	15
2	问答题	20
3	短会话（对话和独白）	15

所有的问题、陈述、短对话和短独白都有由英语为母语的朗读者录制的音频。朗读者就每个 PART 和题目给出指导和介绍。

The recording is played right through. Each statement is read only once but there is a pause of about five seconds between questions to give candidates time to select their answers.

阅读理解部分

阅读理解部分的题号从51~100，分为两个 PART。考生有35分钟的时间完成整个部分的答题，可以按照自己的节奏完成答题。

PART	题型	题目数量
4	完成句子	30
5	阅读理解	20

在试题册中，考生将会读到单独的句子或者文本，并回答基于所给材料内容提出的问题。但在试题册上作答将不会得分。

为了回答这些问题，考生将运用关于英语语法、用法和词汇等知识以及整体的阅读技巧。

1.4　托业桥考试题目的语言环境

以下背景和情境经常出现在考试中。但是，并不需要对这些领域有特别专业的知识。

住房	公寓，住宅，农场，买卖和租赁，维修
家庭与朋友	与家庭成员和朋友一起做的活动，邀请，宠物
健康	医生，牙医，诊所，医院，一般健康与保健
态度与情感	情感，好恶，短对话，社交英语

学校	班级，教室，科目，教师，学生，书，家庭作业
办公室	信件，备忘录，电话与留言，传真和电邮信息，办公设备和家具，办公流程和短对话，计划（*日期和时间*）
普通商务	销售，研讨会，会议，培训，账单，银行，约会，广告

闲暇活动	爱好，运动，俱乐部和社团活动
娱乐	电影，剧院，音乐，艺术展览，博物馆，体育赛事
外出就餐	午餐，晚宴，餐馆，预订
购物	食品杂货，服饰和其他购买的物品
旅游	指南，火车，飞机，出租车，公交车，轮船，渡轮，票，时刻表，车站和机场通告，汽车租赁，酒店，预订
新闻	天气预报，新闻节目，报纸

1.5 考试组织

只有经过培训和认证的人员才能组织考试。考生报名参加考试的方式有如下几种：

—中学、学院、大学、语言学校、移民机构或企业为其学生、客户或雇员组织的内部考试；
—通过认证的考试中心的公开考试；
—由遍布全球的托业机构组织的固定日程考试。

如果你所在的单位无法安排托业桥考试，请联系你所在地的托业代表，以获取参加考试的时间和地点。

1.6 考试评分及小分

得分是基于回答正确的问题数量计算的。错误答案不倒扣分。

应试者会分别获得听力得分和阅读得分，两项相加即为总成绩。

托业桥考试中每一部分测试得分都在 10~90 分，因此两项总分即在 20~180 分。

托业桥考试不是一项正式的考试，而是一项语言熟练程度的评估测试，因此这个测试没有所谓的及格分数线。

应试者除了获得听力和阅读测试的得分外，还会获得托业桥“小分”，用以诊断他们的强项和弱项。这些信息评估其在以下 5 个主要语言领域的熟练程度：

—功能性
—听力技巧
—阅读技巧
—词汇量
—语法

小分评级分为1、2、3级，“3”是最高评级。举例来说，听力技巧获得1分，意味着应试者通常难以理解英文谈话或对话的目的和/或主要意思，这说明该应试者目前应着重提高听力理解技能。

所有应试者都会收到他们测试结果的官方证明，或者是成绩证书，或者是一份简单的得分报告。应试者的雇主或者学校也会收到一份得分名册，其中包括：

—每个应试者的分项得分：包括听力理解和阅读理解得分、最高分、最低分和总平均分；

—之前参加过测试的应试者的得分；

—该组织之前考试的最高分、最低分和平均分，和同行业其他组织的得分情况对比。

1.7　托业与托业桥的区别

对于测试母语为非英语的人的英语水平，托业类测试是高度可信和准确的。但是这两种考试的目的却各有不同。

托业考试（TOEIC TEST）用于评估在国际工作场所环境下对于英语应熟练掌握的程度。

托业桥考试（TOEIC BRIDGE TEST）以托业考试为基础，但问题相对更容易，因为托业桥是为英语初学者及中低水平者设计的。它适合于学生以及使用英语工作或旅行的人。

	托业	托业桥
目的	评估在国际工作场所环境下对于英语应熟练掌握的程度	衡量在一般性工作场所环境下的英语水平
等级	中级至基本精通水平	初学者至中低水平
适用人群	**学生**：普通高校、专业技术学院、工商院校 **职员**：需要在国际环境中运营的公司 **个人及求职者**：需要具有国际认证的英语等级证书	**学生**：中学、大专院校 **职员**：需要在国际环境中运营的公司 **个人及求职者**：需要具有国际认证的英语等级证书

续前表

	托业	托业桥
适用机构	**大型国际集团** —识别语言培训需求并分配培训预算 —测试员工英语是否精通 —招聘、晋升或奖励员工 —确定某一职位需要的英语水平（基准测试） **高等教育机构** —通过设定课程目标提高学习积极性 —持有权威机构认定的英语水平证明提高其文凭的含金量 —可在简历中准确体现其语言水平的信息 **私立和公立语言培训机构** —作为分级测试工具 —客观衡量其培训后英语熟练程度的方法	**公司** —识别员工继续语言培训需求，设定精准培训目标并分配培训预算 —在语言审核时可以比较英语掌握的水平 **中学、大中专院校** —通过设定课程目标提高学习积极性 —监测学生在课程不同阶段的进展 **私立和公立语言培训机构** —将学生置于英语水平相当的集体中，鼓励他们向既定目标努力 —通过可靠的外部认证，保持培训计划的有效性
考试题型	**听力理解部分（*45 分钟*）** **Part Ⅰ** 图片题（20 个问题） **Part Ⅱ** 问答题（30 个问题） **Part Ⅲ** 短对话（30 个问题） **Part Ⅳ** 短独白（20 个问题） **阅读理解部分（*75 分钟*）** **Part Ⅴ** 完成句子（40 个问题） **Part Ⅵ** 改错（20 个问题） **Part Ⅶ** 阅读（40 个问题）	**听力理解部分（*25 分钟*）** **Part Ⅰ** 图片题（15 个问题） **Part Ⅱ** 问答题（20 个问题） **Part Ⅲ** 短会话（对话和独白）（15 个问题） **阅读理解部分（*35 分钟*）** **Part Ⅳ** 完成句子（30 个问题） **Part Ⅴ** 阅读（20 个问题）
考试时长	共 2 小时 （+各部分介绍 30 分钟）	共 1 小时 （+各部分介绍 30 分钟）
评分等级	—听力理解部分：5~495 分 —阅读理解部分：5~495 分 —总计：10~990 分	—听力理解部分：10~90 分 —阅读理解部分：10~90 分 —总计：20~180 分
得分报告	—给应试者分数报告或成绩证书 —给应试者的雇主或学校得分汇总表	—给应试者分数报告或成绩证书 —给应试者的雇主或学校得分汇总表

1.8　如何备考托业桥

托业桥考试是用来帮助老师、初学至中级学习者及雇主评估一般英语水平的工具。

准备考试的过程可以帮助语言学习者提高考试成绩，同时也能提高其在各种场合下使用和理解书面文字和口语表达的能力。

有多种备考托业桥考试的方式。最好的一种方式大概就是尽可能地试着练习使用英语，使用不同类型的“真实的”的口语与书面素材。这里有以下几方面建议：

社交方面

—和朋友或同事讨论

—和母语为英语者建立交流小组

—上英语课

—兴趣小组（*网络*）

媒体工具

—CD 光盘和卡带（*简短对话*、*面谈*、*小故事*、*诗歌*、*歌曲等*）

—广播节目（*新闻*、*报告*、*采访*、*广告等*）

—录像带/DVD 光盘/电视节目（*报道*、*采访*、*脱口秀*、*电影等*）

阅读

—图书（*原版书*、*双语版或简写版*）：小说、短故事、剧本、指导手册等

—地方性和国际性的报纸杂志（*纸质版或者网络版*）

—宣传手册

—目录册

1.9　本书的结构

《**托业桥考试全攻略**》的目的就是让你了解考试的形式及考试的目的。

这本书及其配套的音频可以用作课堂备考教材或自学。它通过有效的途径帮助你建立起一套成功应对考试问题的答题技巧，同时也可以有效地全面提高你的英语水平。

下面是本书内容提纲：

第 1 章—考试介绍

本章简要介绍了托业桥考试（TOEIC BRIDGE），说明了其测试对象及目的，同时还比较了其与托业考试的不同。

第 2 章—小测试 1

小测试中的 35 个简短的诊断性问题目的是帮助学习者识别其英语的弱项，从而明确自己在测试中最需要注意的部分。

第 3 章—PART Ⅰ部分的应试技巧

针对考试第一部分（*图片描述*）的复习原则、实例说明及练习。

第 4 章—PART Ⅱ部分的应试技巧

针对考试第二部分（*回答问题*）的复习原则、实例说明及练习。

第 5 章—PART Ⅲ部分的应试技巧

针对考试第三部分（*简短对话*）的复习原则、实例说明及练习。

第 6 章—小测试 2 听力理解部分

共有 20 道托业桥模拟听力理解题，用以复习在第 3、4、5 章中掌握的学习技巧。

第 7 章—PART Ⅳ部分的应试技巧

针对考试第四部分（*完成句子*）的复习原则、实例说明及练习。

第 8 章—PART Ⅴ部分的应试技巧

针对考试第五部分（*阅读理解*）的复习原则、实例说明及练习。

第 9 章—小测试 3 阅读理解部分

共有 20 道托业桥阅读理解模拟测试题，用以复习在 7、8 章节掌握的学习技巧。

第 10 章—词汇复习

这一参考部分的练习包含了托业桥应试者考试时需要重点掌握的词汇范围。

第 11 章—语法复习

这一参考部分包含了托业桥应试者考试时需要重点掌握的一些语法要点的解释、举例和练习题。

第 12 章—托业桥模拟测试

本章提供两套托业桥全真模拟测试题（每套题 100 个问题）。

附录

这一部分包括：

—3 个小测试及 2 套全真模拟测试题的完整答案及其解析与听力文本。

—全部语法和单词练习的答案（第 3、4、5、7、8、10 和 11 章）。

—不规则动词表。

听力文本

—包括本书中全部的听力资料。

—录音来自几位口音大不相同的英语母语人士，从而让听者熟悉多种口音，与真实的托业桥考试相同。

—本书中听音部分都标有如下标志：

1.10　美式英语的措辞与拼写

托业桥考试可在全球范围内适用，但它是从美国发展起来的。尽管这一考试立足于“国际交流英语”，考试的开发者还是偏重于使用了典型的美式英语。所有词条都经过语言专家审阅以确保这些词汇适宜于非英语母语者使用且为其所接受。然而，应试者还是会对一些内容产生混淆。

以下所列单词表并不完备，其目的是举例说明实际测试中通常所见的美式英语形式。

—词汇区别

英式英语	美式英语
Autumn	Fall
Chips	French fries
Film	Movie
Flat	Apartment
Holiday	Vacation
Lift	Elevator
Lorry	Truck
Pavement	Sidewalk
Petrol	Gas
Post code	Zip code
Shop	Store
Taxi	Cab
Toilet	Rest room
Trousers	Pants
Underground	Subway

—拼写区别

	英式英语	美式英语
-ogue → -og	Catal**ogue** Dial**ogue**	Catal**og** Dial**og**
-our → -or	Col**our** Fav**our**ite	Col**or** Fav**or**ite
-ll → -l	Trave**ll**er Cance**ll**ed	Trave**l**er Cance**l**ed
-re → -er	Theat**re** Cent**re**	Theat**er** Cent**er**

上述大多数词汇形式都会在本书中的例子、练习、小测试及模拟测试中使用。

1.11 学习计划

本书的目的旨在帮助应试者以有效的方式来备考托业桥考试。本书可以用作课堂内备考的教材或自学使用。它通过有效的途径帮助你建立起一套成功应对考试问题的答题技巧，同时也可以有效地全面提高你的英语水平。

下面提供两种使用本书的方式。它们可以作为其他相关听力和阅读理解材料的补充。

学习计划 A

第 1 步

—浏览*第 1 章*考试介绍，以便对该考试及其模式有个总体了解。

第 2 步

—完成*第 2 章*小测试 1。这个缩减为 35 道测验题的诊断测试会帮助你快速了解需要强化练习的知识点。

—比照本书附录中的答案、解析及听力文本会帮助你明白错在何处，并从中吸取经验。

第 3 步

—学习听力理解部分的应试技巧，并完成*第 3 章至第 5 章*的练习。

—参照附录答案检查练习结果。

—这三章的应试技巧部分可以与*第 10 章*的词汇复习部分相互参考着学习。老师可以选择这一章节作为学生的家庭作业。

—参照附录答案检查练习结果。

第 4 步

—为了检查你的学习进步情况，完成*第 6 章*的小测试 2。这一测试中的 20 道听力理解题与托业桥考试中的类型相同，以温习在第 3、4、5 章中学习到的应试技巧。

第 5 步

—学习阅读理解部分的应试技巧，并完成*第 7、8 章*的练习。

—参照附录答案检查练习结果。

—这两章的应试技巧部分可以与*第 11 章*里的语法复习部分相互参考着学习。老师可以选择这一章节作为学生的家庭作业。

—参照附录答案检查练习结果。

第 6 步

—为了检查你的学习进步情况，完成*第 9 章*的小测试 3。这一测试中是 20 道阅读理解题与托业桥考试中类型相同，以温习在第 7、8 章中学习到的应试技巧。

第 7 步

—当你已经学习并完成本书第 1 到第 11 章节所有要点时，将*第 12 章*的模拟测试作为最终的检测。

—比照本书附录中的答案、解析及听力文本会帮助你明白错在何处，并从中吸取经验。

—尽管测试不会给你实际托业桥考试分数，但这些测试会帮助你清楚地了解自己在各种场合下使用和掌握的英语写作和口语水平。

以下表格概括了学习计划 A 的 7 步。

第 1 步	**考试介绍**（*第 1 章*） 介绍考试和考试形式	
第 2 步	**小测试 1**（*第 2 章*） 这 35 道诊断型测试题会帮助你快速了解需要加强练习的知识点。	
第 3 步	**听力理解应试技巧**（*第 3 章~第 5 章*） 小技巧，举例说明，练习题	这三章的应试技巧部分可以与*第 10 章*的词汇复习部分相互参考着学习。
第 4 步	**小测试 2：听力理解**（*第 6 章*） 这一测试中的 20 道听力理解题与托业桥考试中类型相同，以温习在第 3、4、5 章中学习到的应试技巧。	
第 5 步	**阅读理解应试技巧**（*第 7 章、第 8 章*） 小技巧，举例说明，练习题	这两章的应试技巧部分可以与*第 11 章*里的语法复习部分相互参考着学习。
第 6 步	**小测试 3：阅读理解**（*第 9 章*） 这一测试中的 20 道阅读理解题与托业桥考试中类型相同，以温习在第 7、8 章中学习到的应试技巧。	
第 7 步	**2 套全真模拟测试**（*第 12 章*） 完成 1 套或 2 套完整测试（每套 100 道题）作为最后的检验。	

学习计划 B

有些应试者可能没有充裕时间备考托业桥考试。这种情况下，他们需要集中精力在考试的重、难点部分。以下 3 步可以解决这一问题：

第 1 步

—完成*第 2 章*小测试 1。这 35 道诊断型测试题会帮助你快速了解托业桥考试内容及题型，还会帮助你快速了解需要加强练习的知识点。

—比照本书附录中的答案、解析及听力文本会帮助你明白错在何处，并从中吸取经验。

第 2 步

—学习应试技巧，完成*第 3、4、5、7、8 章*的练习题。选择你需要着重训练的章节学习。

—这几章的应试技巧部分可以与*第 10 章*的词汇复习部分以及*第 11 章*里的语法复习部分相互参考着学习。

—参照附录答案检查练习结果。

第 3 步

—如果时间允许，至少做一套*第 12 章*的全真模拟测试题，检测最后的学习成果。

—比照本书附录中的答案、解析及听力文本会帮助你明白错在何处，并从中吸取经验。

—尽管测试不会给你实际托业桥考试分数，但这些测试会帮助你清楚地了解自己在各种场合下使用和掌握的英语写作和口语的水平。

以下表格概括了学习计划 B 的 3 步。

第 1 步	*第 2 章*由 35 道诊断型考题构成的小测试帮助你了解需要加强练习的知识点。	
第 2 步	通过学习*第 3、4、5、7、8 章*中的技巧、举例说明和练习题，掌握听力理解和阅读的技巧。	这几章的应试技巧部分可以与*第 10 章*的词汇复习部分以及*第 11 章*里的语法复习部分相互参考着学习。
第 3 步	至少完成一套*第 12 章*的全真模拟测试题。	

第2章

小测试1

全题型

这个小测试是一个快速诊断测试，目的在于帮助应试者了解考试，了解自身英语的不足之处，进而确定其需要加强的方面。

小测试共有 35 道题。

听力理解部分

—Part Ⅰ：图片题（*5 道题*）
—Part Ⅱ：问答题（*8 道题*）
—Part Ⅲ：短会话（对话和独白）（*5 道题*）

阅读部分

—Part Ⅳ完成句子（*10 道题*）
—Part Ⅴ阅读理解（*7 道题*）

听力理解部分的问题都有音频。

使用答题卡填写答案。在托业桥的实际考试中，必须将正确答案涂写在答题卡上才能得分，不能随意涂写。

注意每个问题只有一个正确答案。

比照本书附录 B 中的答案、解析及听力文本会帮助你明白错在何处，并从中吸取经验。

现在，翻到下一页，开始小测试吧！

小测试 1
答题卡

听力理解

PART Ⅰ
Photographs
5 questions

1.	A	B	C	D
2.	A	B	C	D
3.	A	B	C	D
4.	A	B	C	D
5.	A	B	C	D

PART Ⅱ
Question – Response
8 questions

6.	A	B	C
7.	A	B	C
8.	A	B	C
9.	A	B	C
10.	A	B	C
11.	A	B	C
12.	A	B	C
13.	A	B	C

PART Ⅲ
Short Conversations and Short Talks
5 questions

14.	A	B	C	D
15.	A	B	C	D
16.	A	B	C	D
17.	A	B	C	D
18.	A	B	C	D

阅读理解

PART Ⅳ
Incomplete Sentences
10 questions

19.	A	B	C	D
20.	A	B	C	D
21.	A	B	C	D
22.	A	B	C	D
23.	A	B	C	D
24.	A	B	C	D
25.	A	B	C	D
26.	A	B	C	D
27.	A	B	C	D
28.	A	B	C	D

PART Ⅴ
Reading Comprehension
7 questions

29.	A	B	C	D
30.	A	B	C	D
31.	A	B	C	D
32.	A	B	C	D
33.	A	B	C	D
34.	A	B	C	D
35.	A	B	C	D

记分卡

在下面表格中记录下你在相应部分答题的正确数量。这会有助你了解自己的强项，同时重点关注需加强的部分。

PART Ⅰ	---- / 5
PART Ⅱ	---- / 8
PART Ⅲ	---- / 5
PART Ⅳ	---- / 10
PART Ⅴ	---- / 7
TOTAL	---- /35

托业桥 Mini-test 1

LISTENING COMPREHENSION

This is the listening section of the test. There are three parts to this section.

PART Ⅰ

Directions: You will see a picture in your test book and you will hear four short statements.

Look at the picture in your test book and choose the statement that best describes what you see in the picture. Then mark your answer on your answer sheet.

Look at the sample below and listen to the four statements.

Statement (B), “The boys are reading”, best describes what you see in the picture. Therefore, you should choose answer (B).

Sample Answer

(A) ● (C) (D)

Now let us begin Part Ⅰ with question number one.

1.

2.

3.

4.

5.

Source: www.bigfoto.com

PART Ⅱ 

Directions: Now, you will hear a question or statement followed by three responses. Choose the best response to each question or statement.

Now listen to a sample question.

You will hear: Good morning, John. How are you?

You will also hear:
(A) I am fine, thank you.
(B) I am in the living room.
(C) My name is John.

Sample Answer
● (B) (C)

The best response to the question "How are you?" is choice (A), "I am fine, thank you." Therefore, you should choose answer (A).

Now let us begin Part Ⅱ with question number 6.

6. Mark your answer on your answer sheet.

7. Mark your answer on your answer sheet.

8. Mark your answer on your answer sheet.

9. Mark your answer on your answer sheet.

10. Mark your answer on your answer sheet.

11. Mark your answer on your answer sheet.

12. Mark your answer on your answer sheet.

13. Mark your answer on your answer sheet.

PART Ⅲ

Directions: Now, you will hear several short talks or conversations.

In your test book, you will read a question followed by four answers. Choose the best answer to each question and mark it on your answer sheet.

Now let us begin Part Ⅲ with question number 14.

14. How long does the man want to stay?
(A) One week.
(B) One night.
(C) Two nights.
(D) Four nights.

15. When will they go to the movies?
(A) Today at 4:15.
(B) This evening at 8:30.
(C) Tomorrow at 4:15.
(D) Tomorrow at 8:30.

16. What will the weather be like this afternoon?
(A) Windy.
(B) Sunny.
(C) Wet.
(D) Dry.

17. How will they go to the airport?
(A) By train.
(B) By bus.
(C) By taxi.
(D) On foot.

18. Who is Jessica Smith?
(A) A visitor.
(B) A manager.
(C) Mr Sakamoto's colleague.
(D) An assistant.

This is the end of the Listening Comprehension portion of the test. Turn to Part Ⅳ of the test.

READING

This is the reading section of the test. There are two parts to this section.

PART Ⅳ

Directions: This part of the test has incomplete sentences. There are four words or phrases, marked (A), (B), (C), and (D), under each sentence. Choose the **one** word or phrase that best completes the sentence. Then mark your answer on your answer sheet.

Example:

Please turn off your computer at the _____ of the day.
(A) ends
(B) ending
(C) end
(D) ended

Sample Answer
(A) (B) ● (D)

The sentence should read, "Please turn off your computer at the end of the day." Therefore, you should choose answer (C).

Now begin work on the questions.

19. I cannot find my sunglasses. _____ I borrow yours?
(A) Can
(B) Have
(C) Does
(D) Had

20. Do you want _____ to the meeting?
(A) her to come
(B) that she comes
(C) them coming
(D) coming

21. Before _____ his own company, he worked as a taxi driver.
(A) founding
(B) to found
(C) find
(D) founded

22. Do you know the students _____ to the teacher?
(A) they are listening
(B) who are watching
(C) who is listening
(D) who are talking

23. Mr Jones is _____ on the phone but I have informed him that you are here.
(A) until
(B) still
(C) again
(D) ever

24. Our company is larger than_____.
(A) they
(B) their
(C) theirs
(D) there's

25. In this country, children _____ to school on Sundays.
(A) has gone
(B) have gone
(C) go
(D) is going

26. We must concentrate _____ the next advertising campaign.
(A) on
(B) to
(C) at
(D) like

27. All those companies borrowed money _____ the same bank.
(A) from
(B) at
(C) after
(D) to

28. Ms Cooper _____ in 1978.
(A) born
(B) is born
(C) was born
(D) has been born

PART V

Directions: The questions in this part of the test are based on reading materials such as notices, letters, forms, and advertisements. Choose the **one** word or phrase that best completes the sentence. Then mark your answer on your answer sheet.

Read the example:

NOTICE

CAFETERIA CLOSED

Will reopen Monday, June 5

What will happen on June 5?
(A) The workers have a day off.
(B) The cafeteria will open.
(C) The prices will go down.
(D) The school will close.

Sample Answer
(A) ● (C) (D)

The notice says that the cafeteria is closed and will open on June 5. Therefore, you should choose answer (B).

Now begin work on the questions.

Questions 29-30 refer to the following advertisement.

Doobie's corner

The best place to be!

Open Monday-Thursday 5:00pm-2:00am
Friday 5:00pm-3:00am
And all night on Saturday
DJ on Thursday from 11:00pm
Drinks at half price during happy hour 5:00pm-8:30pm

Live sports on satellite and big screen TV

125 Michigan Avenue between Henley and Burton streets
(206) 751 25 89

29. What is Doobie's corner?

(A) A bar.

(B) An office.

(C) A sports team.

(D) A TV channel.

30. What usually happens between 5:00pm and 8:30pm?

(A) Drinks are more expensive.

(B) Doobie's corner is closed.

(C) A DJ performs.

(D) Drinks are cheaper.

Questions 31-33 refer to the following notice.

> **REGULAR DRY CLEANING AND LAUNDRY SERVICE**
> Available daily—except Sundays—from 7:00am to 9:00pm.
> Clothes picked up before 12:00pm will be returned to your room the next day in the morning.
>
> **EXPRESS CLEANING SERVICE**
> Clothes picked up before 12:00pm will be returned to your room the same day by 6:00pm. (5 dollar extra charge per item)
> The hotel cannot be held responsible for incidents resulting from the normal cleaning processes, loss of buttons or anything left in pockets. All claims must be made within 24 hours after delivery.

31. When is the regular laundry service available?

(A) Every day.
(B) After 7am.
(C) On Sundays.
(D) 24 hours a day.

32. What is said about the express cleaning service?

(A) Clothes are picked up in the afternoon.
(B) Clothes are returned the next day.
(C) It is more expensive.
(D) The hotel takes responsibility for all incidents.

33. What is the main purpose of this notice?

(A) To sell clothes.
(B) To inform guests.
(C) To give guests a five-dollar rebate.
(D) To indicate room changes.

Questions 34-35 refer to the following form.

TELEPHONE MESSAGE	
To: Mike OSBORNE	***Date:*** June 17
From: Alison Mc Guire	***Time:*** 3:55pm
Ms Mc Guire from BHS Data Systems called. She thanks you for sending the InterCam contract and the minutes of last week's board meeting. She wants to know if you sent out the new catalog as planned because her boss, Ed Powell, has not yet received it. Can you call her back on 0679 585 98 91.	
Message taken by: **Grace O'Neill**	

34. Who is this message for?

(A) Grace O'Neill.

(B) Alison Mc Guire.

(C) Mike Osborne.

(D) Ed Powell.

35. Which document is missing?

(A) A contract.

(B) The minutes of a meeting.

(C) A catalog.

(D) An invoice.

第3章

PART Ⅰ "图片题"的应试技巧

考试第一部分有 15 张图片，包括人、动物、物体或者地方。

在音频中，你会听到朗读者为描述每幅图片读 4 句话。其中有几个相似选项，但只有一句话是唯一正确描述你所见图片的答案。

学习下面的小技巧，它们会帮助你提高答题的正确性。

3.1 仔细观察图片

朗读者会介绍每一张图片。比如，你会听到："Number one. Look at the picture marked number one in your test book." 当听到这句介绍时，快速仔细观察图片。你要：

—明确图片背景
—注意重要细节
—在 4 个选项里选择 1 个

为了保证观察图片更为有效，针对每张图片，你要总是问自己一些 WH-问题：

- **What**?（什么？）
- **Who**?（谁？）
- **Where**?（哪里？）
- **Why**?（为什么？）

WHAT?（什么？）

→ What is the main subject? (*e.g.* a meeting, a concert, etc.)
主题是什么？（*比如*一场会议、一场音乐会等）

→ What can I see? (*e.g.* a table, a crowd, etc.)
我能看到什么？（*比如*一张桌子、一群人等）

→ What's happening? What's the action? (*e.g.* a man is making a phone call, a woman is cleaning a room, a child is crossing a street, etc.)
发生了什么？什么行为？（*比如*，一个男士正在打电话，一个女士正在打扫房间，一个孩子正在过马路等）

WHO (are the people)?
［（这些人是）谁？］

- Children, men, women
（孩子，男人，女人）
- Their relationship with the other people
（他们与其他人的关系）
- Their attitude, expression (happy, surprised…)
［他们的态度、表情（高兴、惊讶……）］
- Their gestures
（他们的姿势）
- Their position (sitting, standing, lying)
［他们的状态（坐着、站立、躺着）］
- Their occupation
（他们的职业）

WHERE(was the photograph taken)?
［（照片的拍摄地在）哪里？］

- In the street, a building, a park
（在街头，建筑物里，公园里）
- In public transport…
（在公共交通场所……）

WHY(is the action taking place)?
［为什么（会发生这件事）？］

- To explain a point to a group
（向某一群人解释一个问题）
- To clean a room…
（打扫房间……）

3.2　只选择陈述最恰当的选项

正确答案的选择必须要基于你从图片中确实看到的要素，而不能仅凭猜想。一些考生因为误读了图片中的信息而选择了错误的陈述。

即便你可以进行一些设想，但要时刻提醒自己：这部分的测试要求是要“选择一项能最准确地描述你从图片中看到的情景”。

Example 1

观察下面的图片。

现在阅读下面的陈述。

有些陈述是正确的。另一些选项陈述的细节并不能在图片中明确可见，因此类似这样的选项应该被认为是错误的。

They are watching a movie.　　错误

They are standing in line.	正确
They are boarding a train.	错误
A woman is paying for an item.	错误
They are filling out some forms.	错误
They are going through customs inspection.	错误
The building is only one story high.	错误
The sales assistants are helping the customers.	错误
They are waiting.	正确
They are not facing one another.	正确

3.3 要完整地听完陈述

在这一部分和 PART Ⅱ（*问答题*）部分，所有的陈述内容都是由一个朗读者朗读的，而没有印在试题册上。因此，在做出选择前，认真完整地聆听每一个细节是至关重要的。

要时刻记住，你需要选出的是“最好地”匹配图片的选项，只有一项陈述是正确的。尽管有的选项的陈述中有部分信息是正确的，该选项也不能视为正确的。

Example 2

观察下面的图片。

现在阅读下面的陈述。只有一项陈述是正确的。其他陈述给出的细节并不能在图片中明确可见，因此这样的选项应被认为是不正确的。

The escalator is out of order.	错误
Nobody is going up to the next level.	错误
Somc pcople are standing on the escalators.	**正确**
A person is standing in the elevator.	错误
A person is sitting on the escalator.	错误

3.4 介词

介词是在一句话中用来连接名词、代词、动词或者短语和其他词的词汇。它通常用来表示它的宾语与句子其他部分在时间、空间或逻辑上的关系。因为介词增加了信息，所以它显得非常重要，并且可以影响到一句话的意思。

Example 3

观察下面的图片。

现在学习下面关于这幅图片的陈述。注意，每个陈述中使用不同的介词对整句话意思的改变。

- The truck is parked ***in front of*** other vehicles.
- The truck is parked ***behind*** other vehicles.
- Boxes are stacked ***out of*** the truck.
- Boxes are stacked ***in*** the truck.

3.5　同音异义词和近音词

同音异义词指那些发音相同、但是拼写和意思不同的词语（如 sight 和 site）和发音非常相似、通常会在考试中被混淆的词语（如 than 和 then）。

以下是一些例子。方括号中的音标将会帮助你了解它们的区别。

Example 4 

The driver is looking at the car’s tires. ['taiəz]
The driver tires me. ['taiəz]

He’s studying for a test. [test]
It doesn’t taste good. [teist]

The man is giving a present to the woman. ['preznt]
The men present a product to the woman. [pri'zent]

There isn’t enough air in the room. [εə]
His hair isn’t long enough. [hεə]

There are a lot of people on the train. [trein]
A lot of people left because of the rain. [rein]

They’re shaking hands. ['ʃeikiŋ]
He’s checking their hand luggage. ['tʃekiŋ]

They are on the same line. [lain]
They are on the same lane. [lein]

They are leaving the boat. ['li:viŋ]
They are living on a boat. ['liviŋ]

He fell off a tree. [fel]
He felt free. [felt]

练习

Exercise 1

写几个句子，描述你在上面图片中所看见了什么。

What can you see in the picture?

……………………………

……………………………

……………………………

Where was the picture taken?

……………………………

……………………………

……………………………

Exercise 2

观察下面的图片。

现在阅读下面的陈述。只有一个正确地描述了图片，尝试找到它。

They are watching a show.	
There is a car park in the background.	
Some people are going up the stairs.	
A woman is holding on to the railing.	
Two women are seated on a bench.	

第4章

PART Ⅱ “问答题”的应试技巧

托桥考试的第二部分由 30 个问题或陈述组成，每个题后面有 3 个回答，其中只有一个回答是正确的。问题和回答都是录音而非印在试题册上。

学习下面的一些技巧。它们将会帮助你提高你选择正确答案的能力。

4.1 疑问词

这一部分的问题有两种类型（“封闭式”或“开放式”）。能够识别出问题类型会帮助你更容易地找到正确答案。

开放式问题

开放式问题用以提问能够引出特定类型的信息（如时间、地点、所有关系、原因等）。

疑问词用在这类问题中。它们通常被置于问题的最开始部分。因此，认真听取每个问题最开始的单词非常关键。

以下是一些常用疑问词：

疑问词	目的
WHAT	提问事物的信息
WHICH	提问具体事物中的信息
WHERE	提问某地或位置
WHEN	提问某事发生或即将发生的时间
WHO/WHOM	提问人
WHOSE	提问所有关系
WHY	提问原因
HOW	提问做某事的方式

Example 1 

听下面的问题和回答。

When did you buy your car?	*(A)*	**Last year.**
	(B)	In Mexico.
	(C)	It was very cheap.
Who do you want to invite?	*(A)*	Next Saturday.
	(B)	To the restaurant.
	(C)	**My colleagues.**
How did you go to work this morning?	*(A)*	Two hours late.
	(B)	**I took the bus.**
	(C)	25 cents.
Where did you spend the weekend?	*(A)*	A lot of money.
	(B)	**We went to the seaside.**
	(C)	Two days.
What did you send them?	*(A)*	**A postcard.**
	(B)	I sent it by e-mail.
	(C)	I sent them yesterday.

封闭式问题

封闭式问题不是以疑问词开头。它们需要回答如 yes/no、right/wrong 或 true/false 这样的答案。

这种题型在考试的 Part Ⅱ中比较常见，但是在 Part Ⅲ 和 Part Ⅴ中很少见。

Example 2 

听下面的问题和回答。

Can you speak Japanese?	*(A)*	She speaks too much.
	(B)	**No, I can't.**
	(C)	I've never been there.

4.2　推理

尽管识别疑问词是个好办法，但它并不总能帮助你选择正确答案。

通常，出题者会尽量不直接告知回答问题所需的信息来迷惑应试者。因此，你需要从录音提供的信息中进行一些推理来获得结论。

现在来看下面的问题和回答。

<u>Example 3</u> 

What time does the train leave?

(A) From the city center.
(B) I must call the station to find out.
(C) It's scheduled for platform 2A.

这个问题是提问时间信息的。尽管选项（B）不包含相关信息，但是它却是最佳答案。在这个例子中，朗读者不知道问题的答案，但是已经决定打电话给火车站来获取信息。

<u>Example 4</u> 

Why hasn't the performance begun yet?

(A) In a few minutes.
(B) At the concert hall.
(C) I think there are technical problems.

由于提问中用到了“why”，你大概会预计正确答案中将包含 *because*（*of*）或者 *owing to* 这类词汇。

尽管选项（C）中没有包含这些词汇，但它却是正确答案，因为它回答了提问中的“why”。

4.3　近音词

出题者也试图通过在问题或答案中使用近音词或者在答案中重复问题中出现的词来迷惑应试者。

Example 5 

下面的例子中，标下划线的词汇发音相同（或相近），但是它们的含义却完全不同。

Have you ever **played** bridge?	*错误*	The **play** begins at 9:00.
	正确	No. It's the first time.
Where did you go shopping?	*错误*	I often **wear** this dress.
	正确	I went to the supermarket.
Do you want me to **type** this report?	*错误*	It's the same **type**.
	正确	No, thanks. I'll do it myself.
Who sent you this **letter**?	*错误*	I'll send it **later**.
	正确	The new accountant.

应试者还要密切注意下面这几组发音非常相近但意思却大为不同的疑问词。

- *Who* 和 *How*
- *Where* 和 *When*
- *What* 和 *Why*

Example 6 

Where did you buy this bag?	*(A)*	**In Osaka**.
	(B)	Last summer.
	(C)	20 dollars.

When did you buy this bag?	*(A)*	In Osaka.
	(B)	**Last summer**.
	(C)	20 dollars.

有时候，正确答案可能不是一个近音词，而是一个同义词（即与另一个词或表达的发音不同、拼写不同但释义相同的词）。

现在看下面的例子：

Example 7 

What kind of **plant** is it?	*(A)*	She's watering the plant.
	(B)	It's a car **factory**.
	(C)	That's very kind of you.

在这个例子中，*plant* 和 *factory* 是一组同义词，它们发音和拼写不同，但意思却相同。

练习

Exercise 1

尽可能多地写下可以与下面回答相符的开放式或封闭式问题。

1 In 2003.

....

....

....

2 No, thanks. I've already had one.

....

....

....

3 At the Continental Hotel.

....

....

....

4 Only 2 weeks.

....

....

....

5 Not very good. It rained all day.

....

....

....

6 No, it wasn't. I had already been there twice.

....

....

....

7 Because of the heavy traffic.

....

....

....

8 It's Howard's.

....

....

....

Exercise 2

从下面每一列中分别选一项组成 9 道问题。

A	B	C
When	didn't you attend	at the station?
You're	is on Saturday,	something to drink?
Can I	the Eiffel Tower,	isn't it?
Who's	going to pick you up	the Spanish class this morning?
The football game	to go to the beach	isn't it?
Why	I get you	Maria's brother born?
That's	was	with us?
Would you like	not going to	your stapler?
Shall	borrow	tell him, are you?

在下面画线空白处写下 9 道问题，并使其与给出的答案相匹配。

1. ______________________　My husband.

2. ______________________　In 1975.

3. ______________________　I woke up too late.

4. ______________________　A cup of coffee, please.

5. ______________________　　No, it's on Tuesday.

6. ______________________　　Sorry, but I have to go downtown.

7. ______________________　　I'm afraid I'll have to.

8. ______________________　　I've already lent it to Barbara.

9. ______________________　　That's right.

第5章

PART Ⅲ “短会话（对话和独白）”的应试技巧

考试的第三部分由 15 个短独白（通知、报告、广告、演讲等）或者（两个说话者间的）短对话组成。在你的试题册上，你将看到 1 个问题和 4 个备选答案对应每个短独白或短对话。你需要从 4 个备选项中选出 1 个最佳答案。

学习下面的技巧，它们将会帮助你提高正确答题的能力。

5.1 首先读懂问题

每段短对话或独白都提供了一些细节，你要在几秒钟之内分析并选择正确答案。节省时间最好的办法就是设法在听这些对话或独白前阅读每个问题。如果时间允许，再设法读下面 4 个备选项。这么做将能够使你：

—对对话或独白的主题或上下文有一个总体的概念
—识别你要读取的信息类型

如果遵从上面的这种技巧，只要朗读者朗读完毕，你就会有足够的时间在答题纸上标示答案，然后再阅读下面的问题和备选答案。

Example 1

***When** will the **next meeting** take place?*

当你读到这个问题时，你可以很容易地猜到：
—朗读者将会提到一个会议
—答案将会是一个将来的某一时刻或者一个短语，直接或间接地指明某一事件将会发生的特殊时刻

有了这些信息，当你在听对话时就可以设法识别关于会议将何时召开的一些线索。

现在请听下面的对话。

Man: Are there any new messages for me?
Woman: Yes. Ms Simmons called three times this morning. She said that the Committee meeting is set for Thursday at 5:00pm.
Man: Oh no. I already have another appointment on that day.

In your test book, you will find the following question and responses:

When will the next meeting take place?

(A) This morning.
(B) On Tuesday.
(C) At 3:00pm.
(D) At 5:00pm.

听对话时，你会发现若干个词语和表达，它们帮助你排除选项（A）、（B）和（C）。

This morning	▪ 这是 Simmons 女士打电话的时间，没有给出有关会议的任何信息。 ▪ 在这句话中，*this morning* 是指过去的一段时间，而会议将在未来发生。
Three times	▪ *Three* 是指 Simmons 女士今天早晨打来电话的次数，而不是计划召开会议的时间。

At 5:00pm	▪ 会议计划在 5:00pm 召开（即在下午）。

Set for Thursday	▪ *Thursday* 是会议最终召开的日期。对话中没有提及是星期二。 ▪ 有些学生总是容易混淆 *Tuesday* 和 *Thursday*，因为它们拼写比较相近。

5.2　完整地听完问题

虽然在听独白或对话前阅读问题是个好主意，但一定要在听完整个录音后再答题。答题的关键信息或许在对话的开始几个词，也可能在最后的几个词。

现在请看下面的例子。要密切注意回答问题所需细节的位置。

Example 2

> "For a decade, Onyx Corp., the Dutch cable operator (…) its partnership in China for 6 months (…) has provided digital television and internet access to 5 million households worldwide."

- Where does the company operate?

(A) Internationally.
(B) In Europe.
(C) In Germany.
(D) In the USA.

选项（A）是正确答案。公司的运行是 *worldwide*，也可以说是全球的或者 *internationally*。

- How long has it been in business?

(A) 6 months.
(B) 10 years.
(C) 10 weeks.
(D) 5 years.

选项（B）是正确答案。公司经营业务持续了 *a decade*，即 *10 年*。

5.3　试着想象场景

在听对话或独白时，试着通过问自己以下三个重要问题来想象它的场景和说话者：

- **What?**（什么）
- **Who?**（谁）
- **Where?**（哪里）

WHAT?
（什么？）

- What is the context? (a business appointment, an informal event etc.)
［背景是什么？（商务约会、非正式活动等）］
- What is/are the speaker(s) doing? (Giving/exchanging information, checking/confirming details etc.)
［说话者（们）在做什么？（给予/交换信息、检查/确认细节等）］

WHO is/are the speaker(s)?
［说话者（们）是谁？］

- Men, women
（男人、女人）
- Occupation/status: professional, student, tourist, etc.
（职业/身份：专业人员、学生、旅游者等）
- Relationship between the two speakers/between the speaker and the person listening: husband/wife, customer/shop assistant, employee/employer, etc.
（两个说话者/ 说话者和听话者之间的关系：夫妻、顾客和店员、老板和员工等）
- General atmosphere: friendly/professional, formal/informal, etc.
（总体氛围：友好/专业、正式的/非正式的等）
- Tone of the voice(s): satisfied, dissatisfied, surprised, etc.
（说话语调：满意的、不满意的、惊讶的等）

WHERE is/are the speaker(s)?
［说话者（们）在哪里？］

- In the street, in a building, etc.
（在街上、在一栋建筑物里等）
- In a car, in public transport, on a plane…
（在汽车里、在公共交通场所、在飞机上……）

Example 3 

听下面的通知。

Good afternoon. Welcome to AquaWorld Park. My name is Samantha and this video presentation will last about thirty minutes during which we will show you exclusive pictures of some of the best known aquatic species including whales, dolphins and sharks. For those of you who are interested in wildlife and bird watching, join Scott Farley outside the main building at 7:20 for the Exploration Tour.

In your test book, you will find the following question and responses:

What can be seen during the Exploration tour?

(A) Birds.
(B) Whales.
(C) A video presentation.
(D) Sharks.

逐一想象对话或独白的场景能够帮助你记忆其中更多的细节。在这个例子里，你可以想象下面这些要素：

- a water park
  一个水上公园
- a speaker introducing a 30-minute video presentation
  一个说话者正在介绍一部 30 分钟的视频展示
- pictures showing aquatic species (whales, dolphins, sharks)
  展示水生生物的图片（鲸、海豚、鲨鱼）
- an outdoor exploration tour (wildlife and bird watching) at 7:20
  在 7:20 有一个户外探险之旅（观赏野生动物和鸟类）

接下来很容易理解选项（A）*birds* 是问题“*What can be seen during the Exploration Tour*?”的正确答案。

5.4　重复的单词

一些在对话或独白中使用的单词经常重复出现在问题和4个备选答案中。

能够识别这些重复的单词会很有帮助，但是有些情况下也会产生误解。

看一下接下来的例子。

Example 4 

听下面的对话。

Man: I'm David Evans. I have an appointment with Ms Marquez.
Woman: Ms Marquez is in a meeting right now but she'll be with you in a minute. Would you like to take a seat?
Man: No, thanks. I've been sitting on a plane for the last four hours. I need to stretch my legs.

In your test book, you will find the following question and responses:

What does the woman want Mr Evans to do?

(A) Go to a meeting.
(B) Sit down.
(C) Take a plane.
(D) Wait for four hours.

选项（A）重复了对话中的单词 *meeting*，但它指的是 Marquez 女士正在参加的会议，而不是指对话中的女士想要男士参加的会议。

虽然选项（B）没有出现和对话中完全相同的单词，它却是正确答案。女士请男士坐下（*take a seat*）并等候 Marquez 女士。

对话中，男子指出一个事实，即他花了 *four hours sitting on a plane*。选项（C）中，单词 *plane* 重复出现了，但是女士没有让 Evans 先生坐飞机。

在选项（D）中，词组 *four hours* 在对话中出现过，但它指的是男士在飞机上坐了 4 个小时，而不是女士让他等了 4 个小时。

5.5　推理

通常，出题者试图间接将答题需要的信息呈现出来，以此来迷惑应试者。因此，你需要依靠录音中提供的信息进行推理判断进而得出结论。

Example 5 

听下面的对话。

Woman 1:　Excuse me, why is our flight delayed?
Woman 2:　There's a problem with the food refrigeration system.
Woman 1:　I hope it will be fixed soon.

In your test book, you will find the following question and responses:

Where does the conversation take place?

(A) At an airport.
(B) On a train.
(C) At a department store.
(D) In an office.

在这段对话中，问题是关于一个场所的信息。尽管单词 *airport*（选项 A）没有在对话中具体地使用，但却是最好的答案。对话中的名词 *flight* 帮助我们判断出对话发生在机场。

练习

Exercise 1

听下面的通知。

然后画线将问题和对应的答案连起来。

1. Who is probably speaking?
2. Where does this talk take place?
3. Who is Ms Vassileva?
4. What is the book about?
5. When did she win her first medal?

A. A swimmer.
B. When she was fourteen.
C. Her childhood.
D. An interviewer.
E. In Saint-Petersburg.
F. A writer.
G. At the age of sixteen.
H. In Australia.
I. Her career.
J. In New York.
K. Two years ago.

Exercise 2

听下面的对话，然后回答问题。

密切注意重复的单词、近音词和同音词。

1. How long does it take to go downtown?
(A) Eight minutes.
(B) Ten minutes.
(C) Half an hour.
(D) An hour.

2. How much is the fare?
(A) About eighteen dollars.
(B) About eight dollars.
(C) About ten dollars.
(D) About thirty dollars.

3. What does the woman want to know?
(A) The time.
(B) The fare.
(C) How far the museum is.
(D) How to go downtown.

4. Who is the woman probably speaking to?
(A) A policeman.
(B) A taxi driver.
(C) An art dealer.
(D) A street musician.

5. Where does she want to go?

(A) To the Museum.

(B) To the baker's.

(C) To a trade fair.

(D) To work.

6. What is said in this conversation?

(A) The Museum is located downtown.

(B) The Museum is near the baker's.

(C) The Museum is too far.

(D) The man is not fair.

第6章

小测试 2

听力理解

第 2 个小测试由 20 道听力理解题组成，与托业桥考试中的题型相同，用以温习在第 3、4、5 章中学到的应试技巧。

—图片题（*4 道题*）
—问答题（*10 道题*）
—短会话（对话和独白）（*6 道题*）

全部问题都有音频。

使用答题卡填写答案。在托业桥的实际考试中，必须将正确答案涂写在答题卡上才能得分，不能随意涂写。

注意，每个问题只有一个正确答案。

比照本书附录B中的答案、解析及听力文本会帮助你了解错在何处，并从中吸取经验。

现在，翻到下一页，开始小测试吧！

小测试 2
答题卡

听力理解部分

PART Ⅰ
Photographs

4 questions

1.	A	B	C	D
2.	A	B	C	D
3.	A	B	C	D
4.	A	B	C	D

PART Ⅱ
Question – Response

10 questions

5.	A	B	C
6.	A	B	C
7.	A	B	C
8.	A	B	C
9.	A	B	C
10.	A	B	C
11.	A	B	C
12.	A	B	C
13.	A	B	C
14.	A	B	C

PART Ⅲ
Short Conversations
and Short Talks

6 questions

15.	A	B	C	D
16.	A	B	C	D
17.	A	B	C	D
18.	A	B	C	D
19.	A	B	C	D
20.	A	B	C	D

记分卡

在下面记分卡上记录你在相应部分答题的正确数量。这会有助你了解自己的强项，同时确定需加强的部分。

PART Ⅰ	**---- / 4**
PART Ⅱ	**---- / 10**
PART Ⅲ	**---- / 6**
TOTAL	**---- / 20**

托业桥 Mini-test 2

LISTENING COMPREHENSION

This is the listening section of the test. There are three parts to this section.

PART Ⅰ 

Directions: You will see a picture in your test book and you will hear four short statements.

Look at the picture in your test book and choose the statement that best describes what you see in the picture. Then mark your answer on your answer sheet.

Look at the sample below and listen to the four statements.

Statement (B), "The boys are reading", best describes what you see in the picture. Therefore, you should choose answer (B).

Sample Answer

(A) ● (C) (D)

Now let us begin Part Ⅰ with question number one.

1.

2.

Source: www.bigfoto.com

3.

4.

Source: www.bigfoto.com

PART Ⅱ

Directions: Now, you will hear a question or statement followed by three responses. Choose the best response to each question or statement.

Now listen to a sample question.

You will hear: Good morning, John. How are you?

You will also hear: (A) I am fine, thank you.
(B) I am in the living room.
(C) My name is John.

Sample Answer
● (B) (C)

The best response to the question "How are you?" is choice (A), "I am fine, thank you." Therefore, you should choose answer (A).

Now let us begin Part Ⅱ with question number 5.

5. Mark your answer on your answer sheet.

6. Mark your answer on your answer sheet.

7. Mark your answer on your answer sheet.

8. Mark your answer on your answer sheet.

9. Mark your answer on your answer sheet.

10. Mark your answer on your answer sheet.

11. Mark your answer on your answer sheet.

12. Mark your answer on your answer sheet.

13. Mark your answer on your answer sheet.

14. Mark your answer on your answer sheet.

PART Ⅲ

Directions: Now, you will hear several short talks or conversations.

In your test book, you will read a question followed by four answers. Choose the best answer to each question and mark it on your answer sheet.

Now let us begin Part Ⅲ with question number 15.

15. Where does the conversation take place?
(A) At an airport.
(B) On a plane.
(C) In a restaurant.
(D) In a furniture store.

16. What does the man want to do?
(A) Rent a car.
(B) Send a card.
(C) Get a car for ten dollars.
(D) Go to Florida by plane.

17. Why is Stuart late?
(A) He missed his flight.
(B) His flight was delayed.
(C) He got stuck in a traffic jam.
(D) The Chairman has not arrived yet.

18. When will they meet?
(A) This afternoon.
(B) On Wednesday.
(C) On Thursday.
(D) On Friday.

19. How old is the girl?

(A) Six.

(B) Eight.

(C) Nine.

(D) Ten.

20. Where does the conversation take place?

(A) On a plane.

(B) On a bus.

(C) On a train.

(D) In a bar.

第7章

PART Ⅳ“完成句子”的应试技巧

这一部分的测试共有 30 个句子。每句话都少 1 个单词或者词组，你必须在（A），（B），（C），（D）4 个选项中选择 1 项将句子补充完整。

本部分没有音频。

你将展示在英语语法、习惯用法和单词方面的知识。

句子都是以正式的书面英语写成，通常不会含有常在听力理解部分中用到的非正式用语。

学习如下的技巧，它们会帮助你提高答题正确率。

7.1　定义问题的类型

把整句话读一遍以便对句子类型有个大体概念。

然后，快速浏览一遍 4 个备选答案。

- 如果答案选项是在不同意思的单词或词组中选择，则是指需要你的**词汇**知识。你的选择将依赖于你对这句话意思的理解。
  如果你不了解全部单词的意思，试着去理解整句话的大概意思。

- 如果答案选项是同一单词的不同形态，则是指你要选择正确的**语法**形态。

请看下面的例子：

Example 1

Carlo was very _______ when he heard the news.

(A) tired

(B) disappointing

(C) exhausted

(D) surprised

Example 2

Carlo was very _______ when he heard the news.

(A) surprising

(B) surprise

(C) to surprise

(D) surprised

在例1中，备选答案是 4 个不同意思的形容词。选项（D）*surprised* 是唯一符合句子上下文意思的词。*surprised* 表达了Carlo 听到消息时候的感觉。

在例2中，用的是同一动词的不同形态。过去分词 *surprised* 与 was 一起构成一般过去时的被动式结构，即“was +过去分词”。

7.2　前缀与后缀

有些应试者经常浪费数分钟时间试图去理解一些不认识的单词的意思。

了解前缀和后缀的作用不仅能帮助你在这部分测试中获得更好的分数，还可以丰富你的词汇量，提高你的整体阅读理解水平。

辨识这些词缀能帮你用上下文及词源的线索来猜测不熟悉的习语的意思。它们当中大部分都源自拉丁语或希腊语。

下面的列表没有列出全部词缀。它们只包括：

— 一些最常用的前缀和后缀

— 它们的意思

— 一些包括这些前缀或后缀的单词类型举例

前缀	含义	举例
Ante- / pre-	在……之前，在……以前	Antecedent, precedent
Anti-	与……相对，相反	Antidepressant, antimissile
Aqua-	水	Aquarium
Audio-	听，声音	Audio-cassette, audience
Auto-	自己	Automatic, autopilot
Bene-	好，好处，有益的	Benefit, benevolent
Bio-	生命	Biorhythm, biography
Circum- / peri-	在……周围	Circumvent, peripheral
Demos-	人民	Democracy, demography
Dis- / in- / im-	分离的，分开的，否定	Disproportionate, impolite
Ex-	外面的，外部的	Expulsion, exterior
Geo-	地球	Geography, geothermal
Graph-	书写	Graphologist, graphic
In-	在……里面，内部的	Incorporate, inject
Inter-	在……之间（交换）	International, interactive
Loc-	地点	Location, local
Macro-	大的	Macroeconomics, macroscopic
Micro-	小的	Microelectronics, microscopic
Poly-	几个（多于一个）	Polyglot, polygamy
Post-	以后，后来	Postgraduate, postpone
Psych-	精神，思想	Psychology, psychometric
Tele-	距离	Television, telephone
Trans-	穿过，贯穿	Transportation, translator

单词附加后缀之后可以改变词性。下面列表中第四列显示了其最常用的变化。你也可以发现有些例外情况。

后缀	释义	举例	主要功能
-able ***-ible***	有能力的	Understandable, sensible	Verb / noun ⇒ adjective
-an / -ian ***-ese***	来自，生于……的人	Mexican, Italian, Japanese	Noun ⇒ adjective / noun
-ant	从事	Assistant, dominant	Verb ⇒ noun
-cian	有特殊技巧的	Physician, dietician	Noun ⇒ noun
-dom	领域，王国，品质	Boredom, kingdom	Noun / adjective ⇒ noun
-ee	接受某行为的人	Examinee, employee	Noun / verb ⇒ noun
-er, -or	执行某行为的人	Examiner, employer	Noun / verb ⇒ noun
-en, -fy ***-ize***	变形，导致转换另种状态	Widen, modify, visualize	Noun / adjective ⇒ verb
-ess	女性	Hostess, waitress	Noun (masc.) ⇒ noun (fem.)
-ful	充满……的	Hopeful, meaningful	Noun ⇒ adjective
-ism	系统，方式，条件	Fascism, feminism	Noun / adjective ⇒ noun
-less	没有，无	Hopeless, meaningless	Noun ⇒ adjective
-ly	像	Easily, clearly	Adjective ⇒ adverb
-ment	……的行为	Government, contentment	Verb / noun ⇒ noun
-ness	……的状态	Happiness, sadness	Adjective ⇒ noun

7.3　易混淆词汇

在这部分测试中经常会出现容易混淆的词汇。它们有两种类型：

—单词拼写不同但是意思相同；这些单词相互混淆通常是因为阅读者对其中一个单词熟悉，对另一个却不熟悉（有时是因为不常用）。比如：look/watch。

—还有一种容易混淆的情况，是因为这些词之间意思有重叠或者这些词可以用在相关的上下文中。比如：rise/raise/arise.

掌握这些词语之间的不同会很有帮助。

动词	含义	示例
Bring	带某人或某物给说话者（bring somebody something/bring something to somebody）	Bring me some coffee. Bring it to me.
Take	把某人或某物从说话者处带走	I'll take this file to the purchasing department.
Look at	观察，看（微小移动或不移动的事物）	He is looking at the photograph.
Watch	观看正在移动或变化的事物（如活动、展示、电影、电视节目）	They are watching an interesting report on television.
See	指用眼睛观察你身边的事物	It is so dark that I cannot see anything.
Look (+adj)	呈现的状态（关于你所看到的事物）	This jacket looks nice on him.
Sound (+adj)	呈现的状态（关于你所听到的事物）	His speech sounds very interesting.
Taste (+adj)	呈现的状态（关于你吃或喝的东西的味道）	Your cake tastes delicious.
Say	发出声音以传递信息、观点或建议 to say something（to somebody）	The children said goodbye (to their parents).
Tell	发出声音以传递信息、观点或建议（to tell somebody something）	He told us that he was tired.

Borrow	经某人或某机构允许，从其取走一些东西，占有一段时间（borrow something from somebody）	Can I borrow this book from you?
Lend	让某人拥有某事物一段时间（to lend somebody something / to lend something to somebody）	The bank lent her a lot of money.

Make	使某人做某事（to make somebody do something）	Just seeing him makes me laugh.
Let	允许，同意（to let somebody do something）	Her parents won't let her go out.

Rise	上升，向上移动（不及物）	The sun rises in the East.
Raise	提升，使升高（及物）	The government raised taxes by 3%.
Arise	发生，引起（不及物）	The problem arose at the end of June.

7.4 假同源词

在学习一门外语时，如果一些单词能提醒你与你的母语产生关联将是非常有帮助的。然而，一些貌似明显的相似之处或许是误导。

“假朋友”（或者说是“假同源词”）是指一些分属两种语言的单词，它们拼写和发音非常相似，但却有着截然不同的意思。

比如，在英语中“actual”是“实际的，真实的”意思，可是在西班牙语、法语、德语或荷兰语中，发音相似的单词却表示“现在的”或“目前的”。

下面的列表是不完全的，它只包括了几种语言中常用的一些假同源词。

英语形式	词义	不要与如下词语混淆
Actually	真地，事实地	Current, at present
Assist	给予帮助或支持	To attend, to participate in
Canteen	食堂或午餐厅(公司、工厂、商店或学校里的)	A cellar, a trunk
Control	给某物或某人的行动施加压力	To check, to verify
Deceive	让人相信某虚假事物是真实的	To disappoint
Education	在学校或学院获得的知识	Upbringing (knowledge that get at home)
Eventually	最后，终于	Possibly
Fabric	服装，材料	Factory, plant
Genial	友好的	Brilliant
History	过去事件的记录	A story (= description of imaginary characters or events)
Lecture	在听众面前正式的谈话（通常在大学或学院里）	Reading
Library	一个存放书籍或报刊供来访者查询或借阅的建筑物或房间	Bookstore
Realize	开始认清某事物	To achieve
Sensible	有良好判断力的	Sensitive
Sympathetic	理解并关心境遇不好的人	Friendly

练习

Exercise 1

将 A 和 B 匹配，组成词语。

A	B	
UNDER	ESS	____________________
INTERVIEW	DEPENDENT	____________________
STEWARD	LESS	____________________
SUCCESS	GROUND	____________________
INTER	EN	____________________
DIS	ESE	____________________
HERO	ESTIMATE	____________________
JAPAN	ISM	____________________
WORTH	FUL	____________________
CARELESS	POSSIBLE	____________________
IN	APPEAR	____________________
UNDER	NESS	____________________
IM	EE	____________________
STRENGTH	HOSPITABLE	____________________

Exercise 2

从方框内的单词里选择一个填入空格处，每个单词只能使用一次。

SENSIBLE	BOOKSTORE	CANTEEN	SYMPATHETIC	ATTEND
SENSITIVE	FABRIC	DECEIVED	STORY	LECTURE
LIBRARY	EVENTUALLY	HISTORY	REALIZE	

1. Why didn't you ______________ the ________________ on German literature?

2. Employees usually have lunch at the _______________ between 12:00 and 1:00.

3. Do you _________________ this is the fifth time you have been late?

4. The store ____________ customers by selling second hand books as new ones.

5. The most _______________ thing to do would be to ask the receptionist.

6. The Congressman is very ____________ to the problems of homeless people.

7. The _____________ they used to make the bride's dress was bought in Italy.

8. I borrowed this book about Italian art from the public _______________.

9. I studied medieval _________________ at college.

10. After a series of difficult negotiations, he _____________ agreed to sign the contract.

<u>Exercise 3</u>

在下面每个句子的*斜体*单词中选择正确的单词来完成句子。第一句作为范例供参考。

1. The <u>*price*</u> / ~~*prize*~~ of cars has increased by 2% since the beginning of the year.
2. Everybody attended the meeting *accept* /*except* the manager.
3. She is not very *interesting* / *interested* in baseball.
4. The government's *economical* / *economic* policy led to a major crisis.
5. They were deeply *affected* / *effected* by the news.

6. He was so *board / bored* with the movie that he left before the end.

7. Why did you park your *card / car* there?

8. *Wash / watch* your hands and brush your teeth.

9. I'm trying to lose some *wait / weight.*

10. I have already made *plans / planes* for the weekend.

11. Hurry up! I don't want to arrive *let / late.*

12. I don't know what to *wear / where* for the party.

13. I'm not tall enough to *rich / reach* the books which are on the shelf.

14. I *read / red* a novel by Charles Dickens last summer.

第8章

PART V“阅读理解”的应试技巧

考试的 Part V 由若干段小短文组成。

在试卷上你会看到每篇短文都有一套问题和四个备选答案。要从四个选项中选出一个你认为最恰当的。一共有 20 个问题。

短文的形式多种多样，素材通常都来自日常生活和工作环境中。

- 广告（*工作、产品或服务*……）
- 图表、图形或表格（*计划、统计*……）
- 通讯（*信件、电子邮件、备忘录*……）
- 制式文件（*登记卡、问卷表、订单*……）
- 通知和标识
- 报纸或杂志文章

问题大都集中于：

- 文件的**一般**主题或目的
- **特定**细节：地点、时间、人物、成本、行动……

回答问题所需的信息通常都在文件中有提及。但在有些情况下，你可能还要通过提供的细节进行推理以便得出结论。

考试中完成阅读理解部分需要的时间会比完成句子部分（*Part Ⅳ*）要长，因为要花时间阅读短文。一些应试者到时间结束时也没有完成这部分测试，是因为他们花费太多时间去反复阅读短文和问题。

接下来的小技巧将帮助你如何更好地管理时间，提高答题正确率。

8.1　先阅读问题和介绍

在有关广告、表格或通告类的短文里，提出的问题通常是关于人名、地方或者活动时间、组织变化的细节。节省时间最好的方法是：

- 读短文前先读问题。

- 读短文前的说明短句。这句话会提示你短文的类型（比如：*第 99 题和第 100 题是关于以下**培训手册**中截取的短文的*）。

通过完成这些，你可以：

- 大致了解文章的主题和文件的背景。
- 更快地确定需要获取的信息的类型。

Example 1

Read the following advertisement.

> **OLIVIUM**
>
> *Discover the world of olive oil*
>
> - Visit our museum retracing the history of olive oil and enjoy our video presentation explaining its production and various applications in gastronomy, medicine and cosmetology.
> - Half-hour guided tours throughout the year.
>
> **April 1 to October 31**
> 7 days a week
> 10:30 - 11:30 - 2:30 - 3:30 - 4:30 - 5:30 - 6:30
>
> **November 1 to March 31**
> 10:30 - 3:30 - 4:30 - 5:30
> *Closed Sunday through Tuesday*
>
> **Admission tickets**
> — Adults: 8 euros
> — Half price for children *(under 12)*

Now answer these two questions.

1. What is the admission charge for children?
(A) 4 euros.
(B) 8 euros.
(C) 2 euros.
(D) 16 euros.

2. When aren't there any guided tours?
(A) At 3:30.
(B) In October.
(C) On Mondays in winter.
(D) At 4:30.

第 1 题的答案是（A）。这个答案并没有直接给出来。然而，我们可以推断出儿童的门票费为 4 *euros*，因为文中指出成人需要支付 8 *euros*，并儿童是*半价*。

通过先阅读题目，很容易猜测出这部分问题的答案显然是关于**门票费**的。

第 2 题的答案是（C）*On Mondays in winter*。全年这里在（A）*3:30* 和（D）*4:30* 时都有半小时的有导游陪伴的参观。参观在（B）*in October* 也会组织，但是从 *11 月 1 日*至 *3 月 31 日*期间周日至周二（包括周一）没有。

阅读整个广告前先阅读题目，你立刻就能知道文章的哪一部分是你需要集中注意的，因此从那里你最可能找到答案。

8.2 不认识的词汇

一次**读**完整个文章。

不要**停下来**试图理解不认识的词汇。相反，试着找出你知道的关键词和短语。

不要让不认识的单词打断你。有些考生试图浪费珍贵的时间拼命地猜测它们的意思。他们认为它们包含了重要的信息，从而产生一种心理障碍。结果，他们慌乱地选了错误的答案，或者更糟——根本没有作答。

为了预防以上情况发生，可以运用以下技巧：

- 记住托业桥考试要评估不同层次的学习者。因此，一些题比另一些题难是很正常的。
- 仔细考虑文章大意并运用你熟悉的词汇知识，尝试理解不认识的词汇。

Example 2

在下面的文章中，比较难的单词加了下划线。尝试跳过它们阅读文章。你将注意到即使你不认识这些词，你也能够理解文章的主要观点。

理解文章大意能够帮助你猜测难词的意思。

> Within the framework of their policy of improving service quality, a growing number of banks offer their individual or corporate clients online services and analysts predict that by the year 2020 more than 90% of all transactions will be carried out electronically.
>
> Online banking allows clients to access a wide range of financial services directly from home or the office 24 hours a day. For example, they can order check books, be informed whenever cash is withdrawn from the account, transfer money between accounts of the same network, pay their utility bills and invoices.

Now read questions 1 and 2 and try to answer them.

1. What is this article about?

(A) Electronic games.

(B) Phone bills.

(C) Banking services.

(D) Opening hours.

2. What is the purpose of this article?

(A) To inform about online services.

(B) To close a bank account.

(C) To ask questions.

(D) To attract new readers.

答案

1 (C)

2 (A)

8.3 推理

回答问题所需的信息并不总是直接叙述出来的。因此，你可能需要从文章提供的信息中做一些推理（即得出结论）。

Example 3

Read the following newspaper article.

> In a press statement released yesterday, Global West announced the construction and fitting-out of a new terminal located right in the city center.
>
> This new facility will welcome passengers (with or without luggage) who want to check in from 3 to 24 hours prior to departure. This service will allow Global West passengers to choose their seats and obtain their boarding passes without delay.
>
> Services operated by Global West also include a shuttle service by coach to the airport available every day from 6:00am to 10:00pm.

Now read the question below and try to answer it.

What is Global West?

(A) A luggage manufacturer.

(B) An airline company.

(C) A bank.

(D) A restaurant.

正确答案是（B）。虽然答案没有直接陈述出来，你可以从文章中给的信息（*terminal*, *passengers*, *check in*, *departure*, *boarding pass* 和 *service by coach to the airport*）中推断出 Global West 是一家航空公司。

8.4　重复的单词

阅读理解文章中的一些单词可能会在题目和四个选项中重复出现。如果能够认出它们将会很有帮助，但是某些情况下也可能会产生误导。

Example 4

Read the following sign.

Sorry
all rooms fully booked
until the end of
the Theater Festival

Ring 0805 23 100
for more information.

Where would this sign most likely be seen?

(A) In a bookstore.

(B) A store selling rings.

(C) A hotel.

(D) A theater.

虽然选项（C）和标牌中没有相同的单词重复出现，但它是正确的选项。

这个标牌解释了由于戏剧节，宾馆中所有的**房间**（或者是卧房）都被预订了。

选项（A）重复了标牌中的单词 *book*，但是用作名词，指代一个物体。在标牌中，这个单词是一个动词，意思是“预订”。

选项（B）重复了标牌中的单词 *ring*，但是用作名词。在标牌中，这个单词是一个动词，意思是“打电话”。

选项（D）重复了标牌中的单词 *theater*，但指代的是一个节日，而不是房间。

练习

Exercise 1

看以下公司资料。

SATOSHI

Status	Parent company
Nationality	Japanese
Founded	1968
Headquarters	Kobe
Business activities	Home and personal care products
Number of employees	125,000
Worldwide turnover	$68,000,000
Main markets	Japan, USA, UK, Germany, Holland

KLEMP

Status	Subsidiary (100% owned by Satoshi)
Nationality	Dutch
Founded	1972
Headquarters	Leeuwarden
Business activities	Pet nutrition and health care products
Number of employees	25,000
Worldwide turnover	$8,000,000
Main markets	Holland, Luxemburg, Belgium, Germany

将 A 中的问题和 B 中的答案配对。

A	B
Where does Satoshi sell its products? How many people does Satoshi employ? What does Klemp produce?	• Norway • 1968 • Cars • 25,000 • Holland • Home decoration products • 125,000 • Finland • 68,000,000 • Food for animals

Exercise 2

阅读以下书信。

Hi Lisa,

I'm sending you this message from an internet café in Rome. For the last three months, I' ve been working at the reception desk of a hotel in the city center. It is a demanding job. I have to smile all day and pay attention to a lot of small details. My boss is a very difficult man. I can' t bear him.

Life is so different here compared to New York. It is a lot quieter and the food is delicious.

I' m having a great time, although at first it was quite difficult because I couldn' t speak the language, and finding a place to live wasn' t easy. But one of my colleagues invited me to share her apartment in the suburbs of Rome. It' s a bit small, but it' s full of character and I love it. Each morning I have to catch a train to go to work.

Thank you so much for the wonderful birthday gift. "Cold wind" is my favorite band. I love the kind of music they make—how did you find out? I keep listening to this CD all the time.

Well, that's all for now.

Hope to hear from you soon. Give my regards to your family.

Love,

Kelly

第一列中的单词都选自 Kelly 写的信。将它们与第二列中的释义配对。

Keep	• To have or continue to have something in one's possession. • To continue doing something, or to do it repeatedly. • To cause to stay in a particular place or state.
Train	• A group of carriages connected together and pulled by a railway engine to carry people or goods. • To teach someone some specific skills in order to prepare them for a job, activity or sport.
Catch	• To seize something, especially something that is moving through the air. • To find and capture a person or animal trying to escape. • To get on a train, bus or aircraft in order to travel to a destination.
Bear	• A large, strong, wild animal with a thick furry coat and large claws which lives especially in cold regions. • To carry or take something to a place. • To accept, tolerate, or endure something/someone unpleasant.
Wind	• To turn or cause something to turn. • A current of air moving across the earth's surface.
Reception	• Place in a hotel or office building where people go when they first arrive. • A formal party at which important people are welcomed.
Kind	• Gentle, helpful and caring towards other people. • Sort, type.

Exercise 3

在托业桥考试的 Part V中，你通常会被问及一些文章中提到的信息点的问题，虽然这并不是总会出现。其中一个问题可能是“What is **NOT** included...”“Which strategy is **NOT** implemented...”“Which aspect does **NOT** change...”

当一些考生没有注意到单词“NOT”时容易选错答案。因此，仔细读题非常重要，并且不要读得太快。

阅读以下文章。

> Good news!
>
> This is a special offer sent only to our most loyal customers. Click on the link below for full details on our exclusive price savings or call 0800 525 028. Our customer service staff is standing by.
> You can order over the web or by fax.
>
> If you wish to modify your profile or unsubscribe from this newsletter simply send us an e-mail requesting removal from our mailing list.
>
> *www.intersoft/specialoffers.co.uk*

判断以下句子的正误。

- ❑ This document is a greetings card.
- ❑ You must send an e-mail to get details about the products.
- ❑ Customers cannot change their profiles.
- ❑ Customers have to send an e-mail to unsubscribe from the newsletter.
- ❑ Customers have to call 0800 525 028 to stop receiving special offers.

- ❑ By clicking on the link, customers can get more information.
- ❑ This offer is sent to all customers.
- ❑ Products can be purchased by sending a fax.

Exercise 4

> **Skilled professional carpenter**, residential building to commercial construction, can perform a variety of installation and maintenance works: replace windows, ceiling tiles, and doors, as well as change locks, mend broken desks, cabinets, chairs, etc.
>
> High quality service, 7 days a week, at the cheapest rate
> For free estimates call
> Nathan Sutherland
> (728) 482 96 00

将 A 中的问题和 B 中的答案配对。

A	B
What kind of document is this?	• An evaluation of the cost. • No service on weekends. • A newspaper article. • Furniture repairs. • A form. • Prices are high. • An advertisement. • An invitation card. • A free desk. • Ceiling tiles. • Furniture sale. • A chair.
What is mentioned?	
What do you get if you call?	

第9章

小测试 3

阅读理解

第三部分的小测试由 20 道与托业桥考试中同类型的阅读题组成，用以温习在第 7 章和第 8 章学到的应试技巧。

- 完成句子（10 道题）
- 阅读理解（10 道题）

使用答题卡填写答案。在托业桥的实际考试中，必须将正确答案涂写在答题卡上才能得分，不能随意涂写。

注意，每个问题只有一个正确答案。

比照本书附录 B 中的答案、解析及原文会有助于你了解错在何处，并从中吸取经验。

现在，翻到下一页，开始小测试吧！

小测试 3
答题卡

阅读理解部分

PART Ⅳ
Incomplete Sentences
10 questions

1.	A	B	C	D
2.	A	B	C	D
3.	A	B	C	D
4.	A	B	C	D
5.	A	B	C	D
6.	A	B	C	D
7.	A	B	C	D
8.	A	B	C	D
9.	A	B	C	D
10.	A	B	C	D

PART Ⅴ
Reading Comprehension
10 questions

11.	A	B	C	D
12.	A	B	C	D
13.	A	B	C	D
14.	A	B	C	D
15.	A	B	C	D
16.	A	B	C	D
17.	A	B	C	D
18.	A	B	C	D
19.	A	B	C	D
20.	A	B	C	D

记分卡

在下面记分卡上记录你在相应部分答题的正确数量。这会有助你了解自己的强项，同时确定需加强的部分。

PART Ⅳ	**---- / 10**
PART Ⅴ	**---- / 10**
TOTAL	**---- / 20**

托业桥 Mini-test 3

READING

This is the reading section of the test. There are two parts to this section.

PART Ⅳ

Directions: This part of the test has incomplete sentences. There are four words or phrases, marked (A), (B), (C), and (D), under each sentence. Choose the **one** word or phrase that best completes the sentence. Then mark your answer on your answer sheet.

Example:

Please turn off your computer at the _____ of the day.

(A) ends
(B) ending
(C) end
(D) ended

Sample Answer
(A) (B) ● (D)

The sentence should read, "Please turn off your computer at the end of the day." Therefore, you should choose answer (C).

Now begin work on the questions.

1. Do you agree _____ me at all?

(A) with
(B) at
(C) to
(D) for

2. Sales will not increase _____ we launch a more competitive product.

(A) unless

(B) however

(C) although

(D) since

3. The flight was canceled _____ the snow.

(A) despite

(B) because of

(C) instead of

(D) whereas

4. Have you _____ been to India?

(A) ever

(B) never

(C) either

(D) again

5. I have just received an _____ from one of our suppliers.

(A) advice

(B) information

(C) form

(D) invoice

6. Many people are not very _____ in politics.

(A) bored

(B) boring

(C) interested

(D) interesting

7. If you _____ your passport, you must report it to the police.

(A) lose

(B) loose

(C) loses

(D) loss

8. I am having lunch with the new _____ manager next Tuesday at 10:00.

(A) person

(B) personal

(C) personnel

(D) personality

9. When _____ work?

(A) does Luke usually start

(B) Luke usually starts

(C) Luke usually does

(D) Luke usually

10. My new car is expensive but _____.

(A) economy

(B) economic

(C) economical

(D) economically

PART Ⅴ

Directions: The questions in this part of the test are based on reading materials such as notices, letters, forms, and advertisements. Choose the **one** word or phrase that best completes the sentence. Then mark your answer on your answer sheet.

Read the example:

NOTICE

CAFETERIA CLOSED

Will reopen Monday, June 5

What will happen on June 5?

(A) The workers have a day off.
(B) The cafeteria will open.
(C) The prices will go down.
(D) The school will close.

Sample Answer
(A) ● (C) (D)

The notice says that the cafeteria is closed and will open on June 5. Therefore, you should choose answer (B).

Now begin work on the questions.

Questions 11-14 refer to the following advertisement.

Assistant Magazine Editor

Are you creative, highly efficient with excellent inter-personal skills?

We are an international publishing group which has attained leadership through a history of professionalism and integrity.
We are committed to hiring and training candidates with a strong desire to learn and grow, both personally and professionally.
We are presently looking for an assistant magazine editor. The successful candidate must possess a college degree in journalism or a related qualification and at least three years of magazine/newspaper experience. Excellent knowledge of word processing and publishing-related software is essential. Must be well-organized, deadline-oriented, with strong attention to details. Fluency in English and at least two other foreign languages required.

Apply with CV and cover letter to:
Linda Morris
ABC international
Department of Human Resources
1368 Riverside Road
Houston, TX 77093

11. For whom is this document intended?
(A) Human resources managers.
(B) Software designers.
(C) Language teachers.
(D) Job applicants.

12. What is required to be successful?
(A) A good physical appearance.
(B) Less than three years' experience.
(C) Knowledge of several languages.
(D) A driver's license.

13. What is said about the company?

(A) It is deadline-oriented.

(B) It has a leading position in its field.

(C) It publishes a history magazine.

(D) It develops software.

14. How can candidates apply for the position?

(A) By mail.

(B) By e-mail.

(C) By fax.

(D) By phone.

Questions 15-17 refer to the following survey.

Name: Frank Shepard
Address: 52 Hampton Street
Allentown

Please answer the following questions as fully as you can to help us plan and improve future exam sessions.
Thank you for your contribution.

1 What is your primary reason for taking this exam?
Required by my company

2 How satisfied are you with the appropriateness of the exam preparation course you followed?

✓ Satisfied　　Neutral　　Dissatisfied

3 Would you recommend this preparation course to colleagues or contacts within your industry?

✓ Yes　　No　　Not sure

4 How many hours did you spend preparing for this exam?
0 – 2　　(3 – 10)　　11 – 20　　21 – 30　　more

5 Who paid for your exam registration fees for the preparation course and the examination?
My company

15. What is the purpose of this form?
(A) To cancel an exam session.
(B) To collect information.
(C) To announce the date of an exam.
(D) To answer questions.

16. Who is it intended for?

(A) Test takers.

(B) Supervisors.

(C) Teachers.

(D) Industrialists.

17. What can be implied about Frank Shepard?

(A) He has already taken the exam twice.

(B) He is not a student.

(C) He organized the exam session.

(D) He paid his registration fees.

Questions 18-20 refer to the following checklist.

▪ **To Do List**

October 14

- ✓ Check my e-mail box
- ✓ Cancel the product presentation
- ✓ Reserve a taxi for tomorrow (6:30am)
- ✓ Confirm next week's meeting in London
- ✓ Phone François Leclerc (do it 1st thing in the morning)
- ✓ Book room at the Imperial Hotel
- ✓ Business Lunch with Mr Tanaka
- ✓ Buy flowers for Susana
- ✓ Expect Mr Müller to ring up at 10:30 sharp

18. What kind of information is mentioned in this document?

(A) Details of a train reservation.

(B) Tasks to be completed.

(C) Phone numbers.

(D) Book titles.

19. What is planned for today?

(A) A meeting in London.

(B) A presentation.

(C) A hotel reservation.

(D) A business dinner.

20. Who will phone this morning?

(A) Mr Leclerc.

(B) Mr Müller.

(C) Susana.

(D) Mr Tanaka.

第 10 章

词汇复习

10.1　住房

EXERCISE 1

1. The landlady asked me to sign the ______ by the end of the week.
   (A) agreeing
   (B) accepting
   (C) leads
   (D) lease

2. The only ______ he has in his office is a chair and a desk.
   (A) furniture
   (B) stool
   (C) stamp
   (D) luggage

3. They ______ a house by the sea for the weekend.
   (A) builds
   (B) meet
   (C) rented
   (D) looked at

4. Wine is usually kept in a ______.
   (A) collar
   (B) cellar
   (C) cell
   (D) ceiling

5. The guard asked them not to lean against the ______.
   (A) argument
   (B) railing
   (C) a wall
   (D) lesson

6. The man climbed onto the ______ to repair the chimney.
   (A) basement
   (B) roof
   (C) fireplace
   (D) grass

7. A ______ was used to lift the heavy containers off the cargo ship.
   (A) crack
   (B) crane
   (C) cradle
   (D) crate

8. We will ______ our new house this weekend.
   (A) move into
   (B) move out
   (C) remove
   (D) move away

9. They asked a plumber to install ______ all over the house.
   (A) furniture
   (B) computers
   (C) pipes
   (D) a washing machine

10. They usually prepare and eat breakfast in the ______ or the dining room.
   (A) bedroom
   (B) kitchen
   (C) bathroom
   (D) hall

EXERCISE 2

请找出下面这些单词中与其他不同的一个。

Kitchen		Owner		Lock
	Furniture		Bedroom	
Railing		Rent		Roof
	Floor		Railway	

10.2　家庭与朋友

EXERCISE 3

1. Brenda ______Robert twenty-five years ago.

(A) married
(B) got married
(C) got engaged
(D) has been married

2. All his friends say that he has an ______ personality.

(A) friendship
(B) informally
(C) nicely
(D) outgoing

3. Young people do not always show enough respect for the ______.

(A) adopt
(B) elderly
(C) educate
(D) inherit

4. Carla is ______ a baby. It is due in August.

(A) attending
(B) waiting
(C) expecting
(D) pregnant

5. They had three cats, two dogs and many other ______.

(A) pits
(B) pets
(C) pats
(D) puts

6. The ceremony will be ______at St Luke's Church.

(A) take place
(B) organizing
(C) held
(D) occur

7. Antonio was ______ by his grandmother.

(A) grown up
(B) been supported
(C) brought up
(D) raising

8. He hopes she will come back, but he is ______ himself.

(A) disappointed
(B) deceiving
(C) deception
(D) lying

9. He is very shy. He does not ______ friends easily.

(A) strike up
(B) do
(C) make
(D) listen

10. Mark and Karen have just ______.

(A) born
(B) bred
(C) brought up
(D) split up

EXERCISE 4

完成表格。

VERB	NOUN
Bring up	
	Education
Inherit	
	Marriage
Be born	
	Engagement
Live	
	Divorce
Adopt	

10.3　健康

EXERCISE 5

1. Josh ______ his leg in a skiing accident.

(A) break
(B) broke
(C) braked
(D) brought

2. My son has been suffering ______ severe stomach pains since yesterday.

(A) from
(B) of
(C) in
(D) at

3. There is still no treatment available for this ______.

(A) ill
(B) contaminate
(C) disease
(D) injure

4. She is slowly ______ from the operation.

(A) treating
(B) curing
(C) tending
(D) recovering

5. She would not put ______ if she had a balanced diet.

(A) up with
(B) away
(C) on weight
(D) off

6. She ______ a cold from the air-conditioning.

(A) held
(B) ran
(C) brought
(D) caught

7. The doctor ______ antibiotics and injections.

(A) prescribed
(B) forecast
(C) predicted
(D) preset

8. He has been ______ a lot.

(A) determine
(B) suffered
(C) examine
(D) coughing

9. They were badly ______ in the accident.

(A) injured
(B) broken
(C) wounded
(D) illness

10. Smoking is very ______ to health.

(A) harmful
(B) harm
(C) harmlessly
(D) harshly

EXERCISE 6

请找出下面这些单词中与其他不同的一个。

Health	Sick	Injury
Feather		Painful
Toothache	Pill	Blood pressure
Heal		Fever

EXERCISE 7

完成表格。

NOUN	ADJECTIVE
Health	
	Weak
Pain	
	Ill
Harm	
	Surgical
Contagion	
	Sick
Pregnancy	
	Fit

10.4 态度与情感

EXERCISE 8

1. We are ______ seeing you.

(A) looking for
(B) looking forward to
(C) looking after
(D) looking at

2. His long speeches are always very ______.

(A) boring
(B) tired
(C) bored
(D) upset

3. He always seems to be very ______ of himself.

(A) sorry
(B) proud
(C) happy
(D) angry

4. Ken fell passionately in love ______ Claudia.

(A) at
(B) with
(C) to
(D) from

5. Very few employees ______ to speak to the manager.

(A) suggested
(B) dared
(C) accepted
(D) must

6. I ______ go to the movies than to the opera.

(A) would prefer
(B) would rather
(C) don't care about
(D) don't mind

7. She has always been ______ of spiders.

(A) angry
(B) afraid
(C) sorry
(D) proud

8. We were very ______ at the way he replied.

(A) disappointing
(B) disappointed
(C) interested
(D) interesting

9. She is not ______ joking today.

(A) in the mood for
(B) instead of
(C) because of
(D) ready to

10. She ______ me to read this article.

(A) suggested
(B) advised
(C) said
(D) replied

EXERCISE 9

请将第一列（1~9）中的单词与第二列（A~I）中的反义词配对。

1 Accept	***A*** Interesting
2 Amuse	***B*** Silly
3 Awful	***C*** Blame
4 Desperate	***D*** Hate
5 Dull	***E*** Mean
6 Enjoy	***F*** Refuse
7 Generous	***G*** Bore
8 Intelligent	***H*** Hopeful
9 Praise	***I*** Pleasant

1	***2***	***3***	***4***	***5***	***6***	***7***	***8***	***9***

10.5 学校

EXERCISE 10

1. Why didn't you ______ the history class last Tuesday?

(A) assist
(B) wait
(C) attend
(D) learn

2. As he was not very bright, he had to ______ all his lessons by heart.

(A) teach
(B) write
(C) learn
(D) attend

3. He ______ of school at the age of sixteen.

(A) progressed
(B) dropped out
(C) joined
(D) left

4. He found a job after he ______ from university.

(A) admitted
(B) graduated
(C) went
(D) spent

5. I did a three-year ______ in psychology at a state university.

(A) tuition
(B) classes
(C) course
(D) studies

6. If you don't study more, you will never ______ the exam.

(A) pass
(B) sit
(C) fail
(D) succeed

7. Attendance is ______ for all students.

(A) option
(B) compulsory
(C) usually
(D) hardly

8. Although he has a good memory, this student often forgets to do his ______.

(A) decision
(B) bed
(C) housework
(D) homework

9. He was given a $10,000 ______ to help pay for his education.

(A) scholarship
(B) scholar
(C) boarding school
(D) debt

10. Jerry has an extensive ______ of history and philosophy.

(A) knowledgeable
(B) knowledge
(C) known
(D) knowing

EXERCISE 11

请找出下面这些单词中与其他不同的一个。

Housework	Course book	Class
Spelling		Physics
Essay	Graduate	Lecture
College		Homework

EXERCISE 12

完成表格。

NOUN	ADJECTIVE
Friend	
	Interesting
Theory	
	Literary
Knowledge	
	Proficient
Grammar	
	Educational
Philosophy	

10.6　办公室

EXERCISE 13

1. The reception is on the first floor near the ______.

(A) enter
(B) entrance
(C) entry
(D) interest

2. Can you speak more ______ please?

(A) loudly
(B) loud
(C) load
(D) louder

3. Can you ask your assistant to buy two boxes of paper ______?

(A) clips
(B) clams
(C) claps
(D) clubs

4. Keep all the brochures in the same ______.

(A) draw
(B) drawn
(C) drew
(D) drawer

5. Did you put the ______ in the cabinet?

(A) fire
(B) fine
(C) file
(D) fill

6. Leave your name and phone number. I will call you ______ as soon as possible.

(A) away
(B) through
(C) back
(D) than

7. I mailed the ______ last Friday.

(A) order
(B) ordered
(C) advise
(D) advertise

8. Can I use this phone to ______ a long distance call?

(A) make
(B) do
(C) ring
(D) reach

9. The new ______ is directly connected to all the computers.

(A) fingerprint
(B) printer
(C) print
(D) printed

10. Would you like to take a ______?

(A) set
(B) seat
(C) sit
(D) asset

EXERCISE 14

请找出下面这些单词中与其他不同的一个。

Stapler	Hole punch	Scissors
Paper clips		Desk
Waste-paper basket	Rubber bands	Folders
Eraser		Stove

EXERCISE 15

请将第一列（1~4）中的单词与第二列（A~D）中的反义词配对。

1	Pick up	***A***	Sender
2	Plan	***B***	Receive
3	Send	***C***	Hang up
4	Recipient	***D***	Cancel

1	***2***	***3***	***4***

10.7　普通商务

EXERCISE 16

1. All our files are kept in these _____.

(A) contracts
(B) cabinets
(C) luggage
(D) pens

2. Sales _____ sharply in the first six months.

(A) produced
(B) raised
(C) rose
(D) arose

3. I'd like to make _____ with Mr Hamilton.

(A) business
(B) an appointment
(C) a job
(D) some work

4. This company has 17 _____ worldwide.

(A) growth
(B) increases
(C) production
(D) subsidiaries

5. We _____ spare parts for cars and trucks.

(A) product
(B) manufacture
(C) grow
(D) sale

6. Would you like to _____ a message?

(A) let
(B) live
(C) leave
(D) left

7. The company has a _____ of 20 million euros.

(A) sales
(B) connection
(C) percentage
(D) turnover

8. This software is _____ every month.

(A) complained
(B) happened
(C) updated
(D) worn

9. The conference will _____ at the Franklin Center.

(A) show
(B) take place
(C) hold
(D) discuss

10. His _____ on how to make an effective presentation was very helpful.

(A) suggestions
(B) advice
(C) ideas
(D) plans

EXERCISE 17

请将第一列（1~10）中的单词与第二列（A~J）中的反义词配对。

1	Add	***A***	Expensive
2	Borrow	***B***	Lower
3	Powerful	***C***	Subtract
4	Increase	***D***	Sell
5	Raise	***E***	Loss
6	Poverty	***F***	Weak
7	Cheap	***G***	Wealth
8	Buy	***H***	Fall
9	Profit	***I***	Lend
10	Earn	***J***	Lose

1	***2***	***3***	***4***	***5***	***6***	***7***	***8***	***9***	***10***

EXERCISE 18

完成表格。

VERB	NOUN
Apply	
	Employment
Retire	
	Recruitment
Appoint	
	Success
Found	
	Structure
Appraise	
	Promotion
Resign	
	Advertisement

10.8 娱乐

EXERCISE 19

1. Are there any tickets _____ for tonight's show?

(A) lift
(B) left
(C) lived
(D) let

2. He has never _____ before a large audience.

(A) performed
(B) playing
(C) write
(D) dance

3. Is the movie _____?

(A) film
(B) subtitled
(C) dubbing
(D) release

4. They _____ the Brazilian team 3 to 1.

(A) bet
(B) beaten
(C) beat
(D) bit

5. He first appeared _____ at the age of five.

(A) together
(B) record
(C) out of tune
(D) on stage

6. The football players went back to the _____.

(A) dish
(B) sits
(C) locker room
(D) trained

7. I'd like to reserve two _____.

(A) sits
(B) seats
(C) sites
(D) set

8. She won an award for her _____ in a romantic movie.

(A) acted
(B) role
(C) reward
(D) perform

9. Several of her most famous paintings are on ______ at the National Museum.

(A) vacation
(B) Sunday
(C) average
(D) show

10. He is one of the most famous _____ in the world.

(A) novels
(B) playwrights
(C) plays
(D) composer

EXERCISE 20

完成表格。

VERB	NOUN
Exhibit	
	Producer
Direct	
	Painting
Sing	
	Creation
Write	
	Runner
Act	

10.9　外出就餐

EXERCISE 21

1. She works as a _____ in an Italian restaurant.

(A) waiter
(B) waitress
(C) widow
(D) widower

2. Does the ____ come with vegetables?

(A) meet
(B) meal
(C) mill
(D) mild

3. The meat is _____.

(A) meal
(B) overdone
(C) fright
(D) cooks

4. I'd like to _____ a table for two.

(A) book
(B) booking
(C) reserved
(D) reserving

5. The drinks are _____ me.

(A) up
(B) to
(C) on
(D) above

6. Would you like to _____ drinks first?

(A) ask
(B) call
(C) order
(D) attend

7. Do you have any vegetarian _____?

(A) knives
(B) dishes
(C) cooked
(D) forks

8. Is the _____ included?

(A) charges
(B) tip
(C) drinks
(D) services

9. I'll _____ scrambled eggs and some toast.

(A) drink
(B) have
(C) preparing
(D) command

10. I'm sure there is a mistake in this _____.

(A) bill
(B) tips
(C) counted
(D) false

EXERCISE 22

请找出下面这些单词中与其他不同的一个。

Beverage	Tasty	Medium rare
Well done	Dressing	
French fries	Chopped meat	Wine list
Desert	Course	

10.10　购物

EXERCISE 23

1. What time does this store ______?

(A) available
(B) opens
(C) close
(D) shuts

2. I'm sorry. We don't have any left. We are ______.

(A) out of breath
(B) out of stock
(C) out of reach
(D) out of order

3. I can't afford this watch. It's too ______ for me.

(A) cost
(B) cheap
(C) expensive
(D) dark

4. Do you ______ traveler's checks?

(A) brought
(B) listen
(C) agree
(D) accept

5. I'd like to ______ for this item.

(A) buy
(B) order
(C) pay
(D) return

6. Can I exchange foreign ______ here?

(A) currency
(B) traveler
(C) bank
(D) pay

7. Take the ______ to the second floor.

(A) train
(B) elevator
(C) entry
(D) step

8. How much commission do you ______?

(A) tell
(B) charge
(C) asking
(D) consult

9. I need a ______ for this postcard.

(A) money
(B) package
(C) stamp
(D) mail

10. What ______ is this dress?

(A) size
(B) sign
(C) short
(D) tight

EXERCISE 24

在下面每个句子的斜体单词中选择正确的单词。第一句作为范例供参考。

1. She bought several expensive *items* / ~~*luggage*~~ at the new department store.
2. As she is a good customer, the salesman gave her a 5% *prize / discount*.
3. She *borrowed / lent* money from her best friends to pay for her apartment.
4. The fresh food department is in the *cellar / basement*.
5. This dress is too expensive. I can't *afford / pay* it.
6. How much is this suit? I can't find the price *war / tag*.
7. This shop sells antique furniture at *bargain prices / cheap*.
8. Some people spend more *money/ bills* on their cars than on their food.
9. As the blouse was not my size, I returned it to the shop and asked for a *refund / recipe*.
10. Can you *deliver / delivery* two pizzas to my apartment in ten minutes?

EXERCISE 25

请改正每句话中错误的单词。第一句提供了范例。

1. They're going to ~~opening~~ a new department ~~story~~ in Riverdale.

    open　　　　　　　　store

2. I'd like to buy a sweeter for my sun.
3. How many cost this scarf?
4. Are you agree credit cards?
5. The clerk forgot to give me a recipe.
6. Can I be of any assistant, Sir?

10.11　旅游

EXERCISE 26

1. We are here ______ vacation.

(A) on
(B) in
(C) by
(D) at

2. What time do we have to ______ in?

(A) boarding
(B) enter
(C) check
(D) carrier

3. He told me that my suitcase was too ______.

(A) hardly
(B) easy
(C) heavy
(D) greedy

4. How long is the ticket ______?

(A) expired
(B) ready
(C) vacant
(D) valid

5. The train to Osaka is on ______ B.

(A) park
(B) gate
(C) customs
(D) platform

6. Hurry up! I don't want to ______ the bus.

(A) lose
(B) win
(C) miss
(D) earn

7. I'd like to ______ my reservation for flight 528.

(A) call
(B) cancel
(C) confirms
(D) ask

8. I'd like to buy a ______ ticket to Denver.

(A) open
(B) admission
(C) one-way
(D) aisle

9. Tell me where your luggage ______.

(A) is
(B) are
(C) are going
(D) were going

10. The flight was ______ by two hours.

(A) postpone
(B) changing
(C) landing
(D) delayed

EXERCISE 27

请将第一列（1~9）中的单词与第二列（A~I）中的反义词配对。

1	Land	***A***	Light
2	Early	***B***	Vacant
3	Board	***C***	Miss
4	Outskirts	***D***	Take off
5	Guest	***E***	Get off
6	Arrival	***F***	Center
7	Occupied	***G***	Departure
8	Heavy	***H***	Host
9	Catch	***I***	Late

1	*2*	*3*	*4*	*5*	*6*	*7*	*8*	*9*

10.12　新闻

EXERCISE 28

1. Here's a report from our business ______.
   (A) newspaper
   (B) correspondent
   (C) travel
   (D) news

2. In a statement ______ yesterday, the diplomat denied speaking to the rebels.
   (A) issued
   (B) listened
   (C) said
   (D) told

3. The latest ______ give the conservative candidate a slight advantage.
   (A) engage
   (B) relationship
   (C) announce
   (D) polls

4. It will be partly ______ in the South East.
   (A) sun
   (B) cloudy
   (C) winds
   (D) fog

5. The journalist read the ______ before introducing his guest.
   (A) live
   (B) speaker
   (C) headlines
   (D) new

6. The State Secretary ______ the end of the peace negotiations.
   (A) announced
   (B) spoke
   (C) said
   (D) asked

7. The second goal was ______ two minutes before the end of the match.
   (A) thrown
   (B) laid
   (C) put
   (D) scored

8. We do not know ______ it will snow or not.
   (A) weather
   (B) whether
   (C) either
   (D) never

9. I found an attractive job offer in today's ______.
   (A) newspaper
   (B) magazine
   (C) qualifications
   (D) page

10. He ______ to several newspapers and magazines.
   (A) read
   (B) speak
   (C) subscribed
   (D) listened

EXERCISE 29

请将第一列（1~9）中的单词与第二列（A~I）中的反义词配对。

1 Cloudy	***A*** Admit
2 Freeze	***B*** Question
3 Supporter	***C*** Sunny
4 Deny	***D*** Minor
5 Defeat	***E*** Melt
6 Trust	***F*** Innocent
7 Reply	***G*** Opponent
8 Major	***H*** Suspect
9 Guilty	***I*** Victory

1	*2*	*3*	*4*	*5*	*6*	*7*	*8*	*9*

EXERCISE 30

请找出下面这些单词中与其他不同的一个。

Headlines	Correspondent	To issue a statement
Release	Reporter	
Magazine	Dishwasher	Weather forecast
Latest events	Interview	

第 11 章

语法复习

11.1　一般现在时与现在进行时

一般现在时	现在进行时
—常规性工作 —重复性活动或事件 例如：They often play volley ball on Saturdays.	—在表述时刻该事情还在持续发生中 例如：They are playing volley ball on the beach.
—永久性的状况 —一般的事实 例如：Jeremy lives in Australia.	—临时性状态 —当前的项目 例如：I am staying at the Park Hotel.
—未来的行动（*基于正式日程、时间表、计划的事件*） 例如：The plane leaves Geneva at 10:30.	—确定的将来的安排（*个人*） 例如：He is having dinner with Linda on Tuesday.
—常与以下的时间状语连用： Never, rarely, hardly ever, sometimes, often, usually, always.	—常与以下的时间状语连用： Now, at the moment, at present, currently.

I You We They	play
He / She / It	plays

I	am ('m)	playing
You We They	are ('re)	
He / She / It	is ('s)	

Do	I you we they	play?
Does	he / she / it	

Am	I	playing?
Are	you we they	
Is	he / she / it	

I You We They	do not (don't)	play
He / She / It	does not (doesn't)	

I	am not ('m not)	playing
You We They	are not (aren't)	
He / She / It	is not (isn't)	

EXERCISE 1

1. Don't forget your umbrella. It often _______ in London.

(A) rains
(B) is raining
(C) rain
(D) doesn't rain

2. Markus _______ all our meetings.

(A) hardly ever
(B) usually attends
(C) often attend
(D) at the moment

3. I _______ the bus this week because my car broke down yesterday.

(A) am taking
(B) took
(C) takes
(D) take

4. His parents _______ her to study Latin and Greek.

(A) doesn't want
(B) want
(C) wanting
(D) they want

5. This river _______ into the Atlantic ocean.

(A) flows
(B) flow
(C) don't flow
(D) are flowing

6. Arnold is in Malaysia at the moment. He _______ at the Imperial Hotel.

(A) am staying
(B) is staying
(C) don't stay
(D) stay

7. Listen! Wendy _______ the piano.

(A) play
(B) is still playing
(C) still play
(D) don't play

8. Who _______ you want to invite?

(A) do
(B) does
(C) are
(D) is

9. They _______ grow fruit and vegetables in their garden.

(A) usually
(B) every year
(C) well
(D) doesn't

10. They are launching the new campaign _______.

(A) never
(B) once a week
(C) this week
(D) seldom

11.2　一般过去时与现在完成时

一般过去时	现在完成时
—在过去完成了的动作 例如：Did you get my message? He refused to lend me his car.	—关注过去行动或最近事件给现在带来的结果 例如：Look! My cup is empty. Somebody has drunk my tea.
—经常用于过去某一特殊时间或时期的行为 例如：I went to China three years ago. I sent him a letter last week.	—指到目前为止的状态或动作 例如：I have interviewed three applicants this week.
	—指在过去开始并且还在持续的状态或动作 例如：She has been ill for two weeks. How long have you had this car?
—常与以下的时间状语连用： Yesterday, last (week, month, etc.), ago, in + year, it's time, etc.	—常与以下的时间状语连用： Ever, never, so far, how long, for, since, already, yet, this is the first time…, etc.

I You He / She / It We They	played

<table>
<tr><td>I
You
We
They</td><td>have ('ve)</td><td rowspan="2">played</td></tr>
<tr><td>He / She / It</td><td>has ('s)</td></tr>
</table>

Did	I you he / she / it we they	play?

<table>
<tr><td>Have</td><td>I
you
we
they</td><td rowspan="2">played?</td></tr>
<tr><td>Has</td><td>he / she / it</td></tr>
</table>

I You He / She / It We They	did not (didn't)	play

<table>
<tr><td>I
You
We
They</td><td>have not
(haven't)</td><td rowspan="2">played</td></tr>
<tr><td>He / She / It</td><td>has not
(hasn't)</td></tr>
</table>

EXERCISE 2

1. He _______ a new job two weeks ago.

(A) found
(B) has found
(C) founded
(D) was found

2. It's the best movie _______.

(A) I never see
(B) I didn't see
(C) I have ever seen
(D) have you seen

3. I don't think that she _______ to Europe.

(A) has ever been
(B) have never gone
(C) wasn't here
(D) were

4. He _______ his application yet.

(A) sent
(B) hasn't sent
(C) were sending
(D) has been sending

5. How long _______ your girlfriend?

(A) have you known
(B) do you know
(C) has been known
(D) you knew

6. When _______ dinner yesterday evening?

(A) did they have
(B) have they had
(C) they had
(D) they were having

7. So far, the company _______ 3,000 units.

(A) sold
(B) has sold
(C) was selling
(D) didn't sell

8. Sam was driving back home when his car _______.

(A) has broken
(B) broke down
(C) braked down
(D) broken

9. Who _______ at the party?

(A) did you meet
(B) you met
(C) are you meeting
(D) meet

10. _______ has she worked for that German company?

(A) How long ago
(B) How long
(C) When
(D) Since

11.3　过去进行时

用法	示例
在描述中：提供背景细节	She was alone at the bus stop. It was raining. The wind was blowing.
过去不断重复的习惯或动作（批评）	She was always complaining about the weather.
过去某一时刻正在进行的动作或状态	At 10:30 he was attending a meeting.
有时一般过去时和过去进行时会同时用在同一个句子中：过去进行时表示的动作被另一个（一般过去时表示的）动作打断	We were just leaving the room when the phone rang.
常与以下的时间状语连用： while, as	

<table>
<tr><td>I
He / She / It</td><td>was</td><td rowspan="2">playing</td></tr>
<tr><td>You
We
They</td><td>were</td></tr>
</table>

<table>
<tr><td>Was</td><td>I
he / she / it</td><td rowspan="2">playing?</td></tr>
<tr><td>Were</td><td>you
we
they</td></tr>
</table>

<table>
<tr><td>I
He / She / It</td><td>was not (wasn’t)</td><td rowspan="2">playing</td></tr>
<tr><td>You
We
They</td><td>were not (weren’t)</td></tr>
</table>

11.4　现在完成进行时

<table>
<tr><th>用法</th><th>示例</th></tr>
<tr><td>过去开始的某一动作或状态一直在进行（持续）</td><td>I have been waiting for him since lunchtime (and I am still waiting for him).</td></tr>
<tr><td>已完成的或刚刚完成的动作对现在造成的结果</td><td>I have been working all day (That is why I am exhausted now).</td></tr>
<tr><td>完成时的进行时态不能使用状态动词（也就是表示状态而不是动作的动词）
例如：To know, to like, want, seem, doubt…</td><td>I have known about it since January.</td></tr>
<tr><td colspan="2">常与以下的时间状语连用：
all day, for years, over the last few years, for, since, etc.</td></tr>
</table>

<table>
<tr><td>I
You
We
They</td><td>have ('ve)</td><td rowspan="2">been</td><td rowspan="2">playing</td></tr>
<tr><td>He / She / It</td><td>has ('s)</td></tr>
</table>

<table>
<tr><td>Have</td><td>I
you
we
they</td><td rowspan="2">been</td><td rowspan="2">playing?</td></tr>
<tr><td>Has</td><td>he / she / it</td></tr>
</table>

<table>
<tr><td>I
You
We
They</td><td>have not
(haven't)</td><td rowspan="2">been</td><td rowspan="2">playing</td></tr>
<tr><td>He / She / It</td><td>has not
(hasn't)</td></tr>
</table>

11.5　过去完成时

用法	示例
是指完成的状态和动作，发生在： —过去某一特定的时间之前 —或者在过去的其他事件之前 （经常用一般过去时表达）	By 10 o'clock, she had already typed all the letters. When the police arrived, the burglars had already left.
经常用在： —复述结构中 —第三条件句中	She asked me if I had done it. If you had asked me, I would have told you.
现在完成进行时（见 11.4 部分）用来指一直进行到现在的动作	She has been waiting for the train for 20 minutes. (= She is still waiting. The train has not arrived yet.)
过去完成进行时用来指一直进行到过去某一时间点的动作。	She had been waiting for 20 minutes when the train arrived. (= She started waiting for the train at a particular time, it arrived 20 minutes later. She is no longer waiting.)
常与以下的时间状语连用： after, once, by, already, just	

I You He / She / It We They	had ('d)	played

Had	I you he / she / it we they	played?

I You He / She / It We They	had not (hadn't)	played

EXERCISE 3

1. This photograph _______ by my wife.

(A) is taking
(B) was taken
(C) had taken
(D) was taking

2. This is the first time he _______ a horse.

(A) has ridden
(B) rode
(C) was riding
(D) is riding

3. It is high time you _______ her the truth.

(A) told
(B) tell
(C) said
(D) say

4. He said he _______ to her the month before.

(A) had phoned
(B) had spoken
(C) is speaking
(D) called

5. How long _______ in Taipei when you decided to move?

(A) did you live
(B) had you been living
(C) are you living
(D) you have been living

6. By the time she arrived at the station the train _______.

(A) is departing
(B) had lived
(C) had already left
(D) had been left

7. Stan is on vacation this week. He _______ to the Bahamas.

(A) has gone
(B) has been
(C) is
(D) would go

8. She has been working here _____ 1995.

(A) for
(B) since
(C) ago
(D) until

9. Monica was nervous on the plane because she _______ before.

(A) has not ever flowed
(B) had never flown
(C) was not flying
(D) fly

10. He was tired because _______ since six in the morning.

(A) he worked
(B) he had been working
(C) he is working
(D) he works

11.6　将来时

WILL+不带 TO 的不定式	—将来的事实或预测 例如：He will be away for five days. Production costs will increase by 3% next year. —当时的决定（也就是说话当时做出的决定） 例如："I forgot my wallet. I haven't got any money." "Don't worry. I'll lend you some."
	Will 在以下词汇后面被一般现在时代替：when, while, before, after, as soon as, until / till.
BE GOING TO + 不定式	—将来的意愿或计划（说话之前就做出的决定） 例如："Why are you turning on the radio?" "I'm going to listen to some music." —由明显或现在可见的原因引起的将来的情况 例如：My daughter is not feeling well. I think she's going to be sick.
现在进行时	—两人之间已经定好的约定 例如：She is seeing her sister next week.
一般现在时	—将来的动用（时间表、进程） 例如：The train arrives in London at 6:00.

I You He / She / It We They	will ('ll)	play

Will	I you he / she / it we they	play?

I You He / She / It We They	will not (won't)	play

EXERCISE 4

1. Your suitcases look very heavy. I ______ you carry them.

(A) will help
(B) help
(C) am helping
(D) helped

2. What ______ this summer?

(A) do you do
(B) are you doing
(C) you do
(D) you are doing

3. "It is Louisa's birthday today."
"I know. ______ some flowers for her".

(A) I am going to buy
(B) I buy
(C) I will buy
(D) I will have bought

4. Saturday ______ the warmest day of the week.

(A) will have
(B) is going to
(C) will be
(D) will

5. Please let me know ______ you are ready.

(A) than
(B) as soon as
(C) until
(D) will

6. I am going to call him while ______ on the train.

(A) I will be
(B) I am
(C) I am being
(D) to be

7. Don't miss the bus if ______ to arrive on time.

(A) you will want
(B) you want
(C) you wanted
(D) would you like

8. The airport shuttle ______ every half an hour.

(A) is leaving
(B) left
(C) lives
(D) leaves

9. I ______ tennis with Bruno next Sunday.

(A) am playing
(B) play
(C) going to
(D) played

10. We are going to buy a house when we ______ more money.

(A) have
(B) will have
(C) are having
(D) will be

11.7　条件句

零条件句

· 通常的事实。
· 总是正确的事情。

If	+	一般现在时	,	一般现在时
If		prices increase	,	people consume less.

第一条件句

· 可能会发生在将来的事情以及它们可能的结果。

If	+	一般现在时	,	Will + 不定式（*不带 TO*）
If		I miss the bus	,	I will take a taxi.

第二条件句

· 对现在或将来动作或状态的假设：不可能或不太可能发生的事情。

If	+	一般过去时	,	Would, could, might + 不定式（*不带 TO*）
If		I had his number	,	I would call him.

第三条件句

· 过去的状态和动作及其可能引起的结果。

If	+	过去完成时	,	Would, could, might + have + 过去分词
If		I had followed his advice	,	I would have saved time.

EXERCISE 5

1. My parents will get worried if I _______ them this evening.

(A) called
(B) don't call
(C) had called
(D) would call

2. If you didn't watch TV so often, you _______ better results at school.

(A) didn't get
(B) would get
(C) got
(D) have got

3. She would have rung the doorbell if she _______ her keys.

(A) had lost
(B) lose
(C) was lost
(D) have been losing

4. If they _______ us earlier, we would have postponed the meeting.

(A) had told
(B) had said
(C) would have told
(D) would say

5. If they asked us to make a decision, _______ it be wiser to choose someone from our company?

(A) wouldn't have
(B) wouldn't
(C) will have
(D) if

6. I _______ him immediately if I had my mobile phone with me.

(A) will call
(B) would call
(C) didn't call
(D) had called

7. What _______ if he had asked you?

(A) would you have done
(B) you would have done
(C) will you do
(D) you would do

8. They never thought it _______ again.

(A) would happen
(B) happens
(C) will happen
(D) happening

9. If you stopped doing it, they _______ be very disappointed.

(A) would have
(B) would
(C) will
(D) had

10. I _______ spend the weekend at the seaside.

(A) like
(B) would like to
(C) look like
(D) would have

11.8　动名词与不定式

后跟-*ing* 形式的主要动词

admit	enjoy	justify	recommend
avoid	finish	(dis)like	risk
consider	hate	love	suggest
delay	imagine	mind	
deny	involve	postpone	

后跟“to”+ 不定式的主要动词

afford	deserve	neglect	threaten
agree	expect	offer	train
appear	guarantee	plan	want
arrange	hesitate	pretend	would like
claim	hope	promise	
decide	learn	refuse	
demand	manage	tend	

主动词后跟-ing 形式或“to”+ 不定式：意思不同

Remember	▪ She remembers locking.（＝她记得她做过） ▪ She remembered to lock the door.（＝她记得她应该做这件事，然后她做了）
Forget	▪ She will never forget visiting Egypt.（＝去埃及的旅行将会永远留在她的记忆中） ▪ I will not forget to call you when I have more details.（＝我一定会给你打电话的）
Stop	▪ When the phone rang, Tom stopped reading his newspaper.（＝他正在读报纸，但是他停了下来，因为他想去接电话） ▪ He stopped to make a phone call.（＝他停下正在做的事，为了去打电话）
Regret	▪ I regret shouting at him.（＝我对他大喊大叫，现在我后悔了） ▪ I regret to inform you (that) you didn't pass the exam.（＝我很抱歉跟你说这些）
Try	▪ I tried to call him twice but there was no reply.（＝我努力去联系他，但是都没有成功） ▪ Try entering the password again.（＝再做一次试试看，没准这一次能帮助你解决问题）

EXERCISE 6

1. She finished ______ the report during the weekend.

(A) type
(B) to type
(C) typing
(D) typed

2. If you have a headache, try ______ an aspirin.

(A) to take
(B) taking
(C) take
(D) about taking

3. He promised ______ me a car if I passed the exam.

(A) buy
(B) to buy
(C) buying
(D) to buying

4. Do you want ______ to the shopping center with me?

(A) to go
(B) going
(C) to have gone
(D) to going

5. I remember ______ the door this morning when I left.

(A) to lock
(B) to have locked
(C) locking
(D) lock

6. She pretended ______ too tired to go to the party.

(A) being
(B) to be
(C) be
(D) to being

7. He asked them ______ a little longer.

(A) wait
(B) to wait
(C) waiting
(D) not wait

8. He suggested ______ her out to dinner.

(A) me to take
(B) to take
(C) taking
(D) take

9. I would like ______ you to our awards banquet.

(A) invite
(B) to invite
(C) inviting
(D) have invited

10. The burglar denied ______ the jewels.

(A) steel
(B) steal
(C) to steal
(D) stealing

11.9　介词

以下表格没有列出全部介词。只是包括了一些最常用的动词或形容词和通常跟随其后的介词。

About

To be sorry	
To be worried	
To complain	
To think	

Of

To approve	To be short
To be afraid	To be tired
To be aware	To be in charge
To be guilty	To think
To be proud	

At

To be surprised
To laugh

On

To depend
To live

For

To apologize
To forgive (*somebody for something*)
To be responsible
To wait
A need (*for something*)
A reason (*for something*)

To

Similar
Superior
To listen
To be able (*to* + *inf.*)
To be accustomed (*to* + *ING*)
To be / get used (*to* + *ING*)
To look forward (*to* + *ING*)

From

To be different
To borrow
To recover
To suffer

With

To agree	To be charged
To compare	To be crowded
To be acquainted	To be satisfied
To be bored	To be happy

In

To be interested
To succeed

No preposition

To access	To discuss
To enter	To phone
To have difficulty (+ *ING*)	To call

EXERCISE 7

请将第一列（1~9）中的单词与第二列（A~I）中的反义词配对。

1	With	*A*	To
2	From	*B*	Before
3	In (to)	*C*	Off
4	On	*D*	In front of
5	Down	*E*	Up
6	Above	*F*	Without
7	Against	*G*	For
8	After	*H*	Out (of)
9	Behind	*I*	Below

1	*2*	*3*	*4*	*5*	*6*	*7*	*8*	*9*

EXERCISE 8

1. Keiko is very angry ______ her daughter.

(A) of
(B) for
(C) after
(D) with

2. I'm thinking _____ my old car.

(A) to sell
(B) of selling
(C) sell
(D) of to sell

3. He succeeded ______ the problem.

(A) in solving
(B) solving
(C) to solve
(D) solve

4. I am not responsible ______ what happened.

(A) of
(B) for
(C) with
(D) in

5. He is quite aware ______ the problem.

(A) with
(B) from
(C) for
(D) of

6. I am not interested ______ politics.

(A) in
(B) to
(C) at
(D) on

7. I'm afraid I can't agree ______ you there.

(A) at
(B) with
(C) for
(D) of

8. It depends ______ your test scores.

(A) of
(B) from
(C) by
(D) on

9. They borrowed $10,000 ______ the bank.

(A) by
(B) to
(C) from
(D) of

10. Their educational system is different ______ ours.

(A) of
(B) from
(C) at
(D) on

11.10　冠词

不定冠词：A/AN

非特定的单数可数名词	There is a bank near the restaurant.
不认识的人	A Mr Jones left two messages for you.
工作的名称	James is a doctor.
度量的表示	He travels to California twice a year.

定冠词：THE

指某一特殊事物或人	I had lunch in a new restaurant. The waitress was rude but the food was delicious.
特定国家的人群	The Dutch; the Americans; the Koreans
人或事物的分类	The homeless; the unemployed; the Democrats; the Protestants
头衔（用于当后面没有跟随名字时）	The President; the Queen; the Pope *but* President Lincoln, Queen Victoria, Pope John Paul Ⅱ
形容词最高级	The largest; the best; the most expensive
独一无二的事物	The Moon; the Earth; the Universe
地理名称	• 国家（集体名词或复数形式）：the UK, the Philippines • 河流：the Thames • 山脉：the Alps • 海洋：the Atlantic

零冠词

指通常的事物或人	Banks are closed on Sundays. Tea is served at 5:00.
地理名称	国家（非集体名词或复数形式）：Spain, Denmark 街道：Oxford Street

EXERCISE 9

1. I read _______ interesting book last summer.

(A) an
(B) a
(C) these
(D) several

2. She goes to Ireland twice _____ year.

(A) by
(B) the
(C) a
(D) an

3. Did you taste _______ cake she made?

(A) an
(B) the
(C) same
(D) both

4. It costs about 10 dollars ______.

(A) week
(B) a week
(C) the week
(D) last week

5. We usually have _______ at 8:00.

(A) breakfast
(B) the breakfast
(C) for breakfast
(D) after breakfast

6. Have you ever been _______ Egypt?

(A) an
(B) the
(C) to
(D) in

7. I need _______ about the project.

(A) some information
(B) an information
(C) of information
(D) for information

8. It's _______ journey.

(A) seven hours
(B) the seven hours
(C) seven o'clock
(D) a seven-hour

9. _______ drink a lot of water.

(A) The French
(B) French
(C) A Frenchman
(D) A Frenchwoman

10. They collected money to help _______.

(A) the poor
(B) poor man
(C) poorly
(D) poor

11.11 代词与形容词

主格代词	宾格代词
I	Me
You	You
He	Him
She	Her
It	It
We	Us
They	Them

所有格形容词	所有格名词
My	Mine
Your	Yours
His	His
Her	Hers
Its	Its
Our	Ours
Their	Theirs

反身代词
Myself
Yourself Yourselves (plural)
Himself
Herself
Itself
Ourselves
Themselves

Examples

- They want to meet us but we don't want to meet them.
- These shoes are my shoes. These shoes are mine.
- She looked at herself in the mirror.

EACH OTHER / ONE ANOTHER

"Each other" 用于特指两个人：

- Tom and Jennifer looked at each other furiously.

"One another" 用于指三个或以上的人：

- The twenty students attending the lecture looked at one another blankly.

两个短语都可用于没有明确的上下文时。

EXERCISE 10

1. Are these clothes ______?

(A) his
(B) here's
(C) at him
(D) he's

2. Luke and Vicky phone ______ every evening.

(A) himself
(B) themselves
(C) each other
(D) they

3. Is Greg a friend ______?

(A) to your
(B) at you
(C) your
(D) of yours

4. My boyfriend and ______ first met at a party.

(A) I
(B) Me
(C) Mine
(D) Ourselves

5. I spoke to the President ______.

(A) him
(B) himself
(C) he
(D) each other

6. Jerry, are you enjoying ______ this evening?

(A) yourselves
(B) yourself
(C) you
(D) yours

7. Can you give ______ a glass of water?

(A) I
(B) me
(C) mine
(D) myself

8. Look at ______ in the mirror.

(A) you
(B) yourself
(C) yours
(D) your

9. The door closes by ______.

(A) it
(B) its
(C) itself
(D) themselves

10. All the players were looking at ______.

(A) one another
(B) himself
(C) ourselves
(D) their

11.12　比较级

规则形式

	形容词原形	比较级	最高级
单音节	Young Tall	Younger *(+ than)* Taller *(+ than)*	**The** youngest **The** tallest
单音节（*以 e 结尾*）	Nice Fine	Nicer *(+ than)* Finer *(+ than)*	**The** nicest **The** finest
双音节（*以 y 结尾*）	Pretty Ugly	Prettier *(+ than)* Uglier *(+ than)*	**The** prettiest **The** ugliest
双音节（*其他结尾*）或更多	Famous Beautiful	**More** famous *(+ than)* **More** beautiful *(+ than)*	**The most** famous **The most** beautiful

不规则形式

形容词原形	比较级	最高级
Good	**Better** *(+ than)*	**The best**
Bad	**Worse** *(+ than)*	**The worst**
Far	物理距离 **Farther***(+ than)* **Further** *(+ than)* 额外的，更先进的 **Further** *(+ than)*	**The farthest** **The furthest**

Less...than

LESS	形容词（*原形*）	THAN	名词/代词/从句等

Less　expensive　than　in the USA.

并列比较式: AS...as

AS	形容词（*原形*）	AS	名词/代词/从句等

NOT AS NOT SO	形容词（*原形*）	AS	名词/代词/从句等

As　tall　as　my brother.

Not as / so　expensive　as　in Europe.

EXERCISE 11

1. Life was not _______ it is nowadays.

(A) as easy as
(B) so easy
(C) easier
(D) the easiest

2. She owns _______ diamond in the world.

(A) as expensive as
(B) more expensive than
(C) the most expensive
(D) less expensive

3. He would look much _______ if his hair was short.

(A) better
(B) best
(C) good
(D) good as

4. It's _______ movie I have ever seen.

(A) the worst
(B) worse
(C) as bad
(D) the worse

5. This armchair is much cheaper _______ the sofa.

(A) as
(B) that
(C) than
(D) so

6. Feel free to call me if you need _______ information.

(A) as far
(B) further
(C) the farthest
(D) than

7. Her essay is _________ than yours.

(A) the worst
(B) worth
(C) worse
(D) bad as

8. He lives in the same town ______me.

(A) than
(B) that
(C) as
(D) like

9. It would be _______ if you took the plane.

(A) quicker
(B) the quickest
(C) the quicker
(D) more quickly

10. It's one of the _______ interesting conferences I have ever heard.

(Λ) more
(B) most
(C) less
(D) as

EXERCISE 12

请将第一列（1~10）中的单词与第二列（A~J）中的反义词配对。

1	Older	***A***	Worse
2	Uglier	***B***	Smaller
3	Farther	***C***	Shorter
4	Cheaper	***D***	More expensive
5	Bigger	***E***	Dirtier
6	Easier	***F***	Warmer
7	Better	***G***	More beautiful
8	Cleaner	***H***	More difficult
9	Taller	***I***	Closer
10	Colder	***J***	Younger

1	***2***	***3***	***4***	***5***	***6***	***7***	***8***	***9***	***10***

11.13　连词

当你旅行时，路标会告诉你此时身在何处，曾到过何处以及去往何处。在对话或书面文章中，连接词的作用就像路标一样会把不同想法联系起来。认知这些连接词会使得一些书面或口头信息的结构变得更容易理解。

下表并未列出所有连接词，而是一些最常用的形式。

顺序排列	First(ly), second(ly), third(ly) In the first (second, third) place Before, previously, earlier	Then, next Finally, in the end Lastly
表示可选择	Both…and… Either…or… Neither…nor… Not only…but also… Whether...or… From…to / until or till… Between…and…	Also, too, as well In addition (to) Furthermore Moreover Instead (of)
表达相似	The same…as As…as	Like In the same way
相反观点	(Al)though, even though Despite, in spite of On the one hand…on the other hand	Nevertheless However Whereas
表达原因和结果	Because (of) Since For So So that Therefore Consequently Thus	As a result On account of this In order to
实际上	In fact As a matter of fact	Actually
制约性	If… then Provided (that)	Unless
重新措辞	In other words	That is to say

EXERCISE 13

1. They will not sign the contract ______ we change some of the terms.

(A) both
(B) despite
(C) unless
(D) earlier

2. You can enter the club _______ you are a member.

(A) previously
(B) provided
(C) neither
(D) too

3. She couldn't eat _______ she was very hungry.

(A) despite
(B) although
(C) in spite of
(D) either

4. You will have to work with him, _______ you like it or not.

(A) either
(B) neither
(C) or
(D) whether

5. He has two cars. Both _______ are Japanese.

(A) of them
(B) they
(C) of they
(D) them

6. Leave the door open _______ he arrives.

(A) unless
(B) until
(C) too
(D) for

7. As I said _______ our sales increased by 5% last year.

(A) also
(B) furthermore
(C) previously
(D) nor

8. _______ they decided not to move to Europe.

(A) Despite
(B) In the end
(C) In addition to
(D) In order to

9. The shop is open _______ 9:30 and 5:30.

(A) between
(B) from
(C) both
(D) either

10. I will go to the library this afternoon _______ borrow some books.

(A) in addition to
(B) in order to
(C) because of
(D) too

第 12 章

托业桥模拟测试

模拟测试 1

答题卡

LISTENING COMPREHENSION SECTION

PART Ⅰ

Photographs

15 questions

1.	A	B	C	D
2.	A	B	C	D
3.	A	B	C	D
4.	A	B	C	D
5.	A	B	C	D
6.	A	B	C	D
7.	A	B	C	D
8.	A	B	C	D
9.	A	B	C	D
10.	A	B	C	D
11.	A	B	C	D
12.	A	B	C	D
13.	A	B	C	D
14.	A	B	C	D
15.	A	B	C	D

PART Ⅱ

Question – Response

20 questions

16.	A	B	C
17.	A	B	C
18.	A	B	C
19.	A	B	C
20.	A	B	C
21.	A	B	C
22.	A	B	C
23.	A	B	C
24.	A	B	C
25.	A	B	C
26.	A	B	C
27.	A	B	C
28.	A	B	C
29.	A	B	C
30.	A	B	C
31.	A	B	C
32.	A	B	C
33.	A	B	C
34.	A	B	C
35.	A	B	C

PART Ⅲ

Short Conversations
and Short Talks

15 questions

36.	A	B	C	D
37.	A	B	C	D
38.	A	B	C	D
39.	A	B	C	D
40.	A	B	C	D
41.	A	B	C	D
42.	A	B	C	D
43.	A	B	C	D
44.	A	B	C	D
45.	A	B	C	D
46.	A	B	C	D
47.	A	B	C	D
48.	A	B	C	D
49.	A	B	C	D
50.	A	B	C	D

READING SECTION

PART Ⅳ
Incomplete Sentences

30 questions

51.	A	B	C	D
52.	A	B	C	D
53.	A	B	C	D
54.	A	B	C	D
55.	A	B	C	D
56.	A	B	C	D
57.	A	B	C	D
58.	A	B	C	D
59.	A	B	C	D
60.	A	B	C	D
61.	A	B	C	D
62.	A	B	C	D
63.	A	B	C	D
64.	A	B	C	D
65.	A	B	C	D

66.	A	B	C	D
67.	A	B	C	D
68.	A	B	C	D
69.	A	B	C	D
70.	A	B	C	D
71.	A	B	C	D
72.	A	B	C	D
73.	A	B	C	D
74.	A	B	C	D
75.	A	B	C	D
76.	A	B	C	D
77.	A	B	C	D
78.	A	B	C	D
79.	A	B	C	D
80.	A	B	C	D

PART Ⅴ
Reading Comprehension

20 questions

81.	A	B	C	D
82.	A	B	C	D
83.	A	B	C	D
84.	A	B	C	D
85.	A	B	C	D
86.	A	B	C	D
87.	A	B	C	D
88.	A	B	C	D
89.	A	B	C	D
90.	A	B	C	D
91.	A	B	C	D
92.	A	B	C	D
93.	A	B	C	D
94.	A	B	C	D
95.	A	B	C	D
96.	A	B	C	D
97.	A	B	C	D
98.	A	B	C	D
99.	A	B	C	D
100.	A	B	C	D

托业桥 Practice Test 1

LISTENING COMPREHENSION

This is the listening section of the test. There are three parts to this section.

PART Ⅰ 

Directions: You will see a picture in your test book and you will hear four short statements.

Look at the picture in your test book and choose the statement that best describes what you see in the picture. Then mark your answer on your answer sheet.

Look at the sample below and listen to the four statements.

Statement (B), "The boys are reading", best describes what you see in the picture. Therefore, you should choose answer (B).

Sample Answer
(A) ● (C) (D)

Now let us begin Part I with question number one.

1.

2.

3.

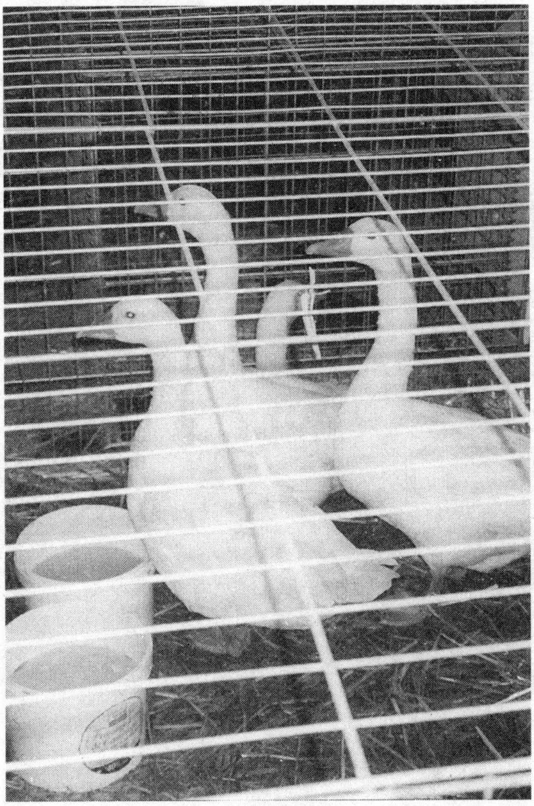

4.

5.

6.

7.

8.

Source: www.bigfoto.com

9.

10.

11.

12.

13.

14.

15.

PART Ⅱ

Directions: Now, you will hear a question or statement followed by three responses. Choose the best response to each question or statement.

Now listen to a sample question.

You will hear: Good morning, John. How are you?

You will also hear:
(A) I am fine, thank you.
(B) I am in the living room.
(C) My name is John.

Sample Answer
● (B) (C)

The best response to the question "How are you?" is choice (A), "I am fine, thank you." Therefore, you should choose answer (A).

Now let us begin Part Ⅱ with question number 16.

16. Mark your answer on your answer sheet.

17. Mark your answer on your answer sheet.

18. Mark your answer on your answer sheet.

19. Mark your answer on your answer sheet.

20. Mark your answer on your answer sheet.

21. Mark your answer on your answer sheet.

22. Mark your answer on your answer sheet.

23. Mark your answer on your answer sheet.

24. Mark your answer on your answer sheet.

25. Mark your answer on your answer sheet.

26. Mark your answer on your answer sheet.

27. Mark your answer on your answer sheet.

28. Mark your answer on your answer sheet.

29. Mark your answer on your answer sheet.

30. Mark your answer on your answer sheet.

31. Mark your answer on your answer sheet.

32. Mark your answer on your answer sheet.

33. Mark your answer on your answer sheet.

34. Mark your answer on your answer sheet.

35. Mark your answer on your answer sheet.

PART Ⅲ

Directions: Now, you will hear several short talks or conversations.

In your test book, you will read a question followed by four answers. Choose the best answer to each question and mark it on your answer sheet.

Now let us begin Part Ⅲ with question number 36.

36. What is the man probably going to do?

(A) Declare something.
(B) Open his case.
(C) Show his passport.
(D) Go on vacation.

37. What is Jeff's problem?

(A) His car does not work.
(B) He must go to the shopping mall.
(C) He broke his leg.
(D) He cannot drive.

38. Where does the conversation take place?

(A) On a plane.
(B) At a restaurant.
(C) At a bar.
(D) At a department store.

39. When is the next meeting?

(A) This morning.
(B) On Tuesday.
(C) At 3:00.
(D) At 5:00.

40. How will the woman probably go downtown?

(A) By subway.
(B) By bus.
(C) By taxi.
(D) On foot.

41. What are they probably talking about?

(A) Yesterday's meeting.
(B) A book.
(C) The rush hour.
(D) A train schedule.

42. When is the office open?

(A) On Sundays.
(B) Until 6:00pm.
(C) From 9:00am.
(D) Now.

43. Where does Mr Nishimura live?

(A) Osaka.
(B) Tokyo.
(C) New York.
(D) London.

44. How will the woman probably go to her hotel?

(A) By bus.
(B) By taxi.
(C) On foot.
(D) By train.

45. Why can't the man speak to Mr Edwards?

(A) He is on a business trip abroad.
(B) He no longer works for the company.
(C) He has moved to another department.
(D) He is in a meeting.

46. What is Cathy going to do?

(A) Get married.
(B) Celebrate her birthday.
(C) Buy Christmas presents.
(D) Waste a lot of time.

47. When will she travel?

(A) At 2:00.
(B) At 9:00.
(C) At 10:00.
(D) At 11:00.

48. What does Melissa want the man to do?

(A) Follow her.
(B) Apologize.
(C) Show her the way.
(D) Go to a meeting.

49. What is the man's occupation?

(A) He is a waiter.
(B) He is a bus driver.
(C) He is a telephone operator.
(D) He is a taxi driver.

50. How much will the taxi cost?

(A) Twenty dollars.
(B) More than ten dollars.
(C) Eight dollars.
(D) No more than ten dollars.

This is the end of the Listening Comprehension portion of the test. Turn to Part Ⅳ of the test.

YOU WILL HAVE THIRTY-FIVE MINUTES TO COMPLETE PARTS Ⅳ AND Ⅴ OF THE TEST.

READING

This is the reading section of the test. There are two parts to this section.

PART Ⅳ

Directions: This part of the test has incomplete sentences. There are four words or phrases, marked (A), (B), (C), and (D), under each sentence. Choose the **one** word or phrase that best completes the sentence. Then mark your answer on your answer sheet.

Example:

Please turn off your computer at the _____ of the day.

(A) ends
(B) ending
(C) end
(D) ended

Sample Answer
(A) (B) ● (D)

The sentence should read, "Please turn off your computer at the end of the day." Therefore, you should choose answer (C).

Now begin work on the questions.

51. I have lost my pen. ______ I borrow yours?

(A) Can
(B) Have
(C) Does
(D) Had

52. As soon as I ______ more information, I will call you.

(A) will have
(B) am having
(C) have
(D) had

53. Did you ______ she was pregnant?

(A) know
(B) knew
(C) knowing
(D) to know

54. We ______ this car since last summer.

(A) have had
(B) had
(C) have
(D) are having

55. When I lived in Hungary, I ______ to take a bus to go to work.

(A) had
(B) can
(C) must not
(D) might

56. Would you mind ______ my questions?

(A) answered
(B) to answer
(C) answer
(D) answering

57. 80% of our electronic components ______ in the Far East.

(A) are produced
(B) produce
(C) are producing
(D) produced

58. The manager and his staff usually ______ once a week.

(A) meet
(B) meets
(C) is meeting
(D) are meeting

59. What are you responsible______?

(A) of
(B) for
(C) from
(D) about

60. When did you arrive _____ the hotel?

(A) of
(B) to
(C) on
(D) at

61. The way of managing companies in this country is very different ______ ours.

(A) from
(B) at
(C) as
(D) of

62. Has she answered your e-mail ______?

(A) last week
(B) still
(C) soon
(D) yet

63. You will have to work _____ if you really want to pass the exam.

(A) as hard
(B) hardship
(C) hard
(D) hardly

64. He ______ drinks any alcohol when he goes to parties.

(A) never
(B) ever
(C) neither
(D) either

65. Have you got ______ to declare?

(A) something
(B) anything
(C) thin
(D) thing

66. The plane was four hours______.

(A) last
(B) late
(C) latest
(D) lately

67. Driving too ______ is very dangerous.

(A) quick
(B) slow
(C) quicker
(D) fast

68. Her husband gave her a lovely ______ of flowers for her birthday.

(A) piece
(B) tin
(C) slice
(D) bunch

69. She has already ______ his letter three times.

(A) read
(B) ridden
(C) rode
(D) rid

70. His speech was ______ than the President's.

(A) interesting
(B) as interesting
(C) the most interesting
(D) less interesting

71. Is the water ______ for you?

(A) warm enough
(B) enough warm
(C) always warm
(D) neither warm

72. I enjoy reading magazines and ______ to some music at the same time.

(A) listen
(B) to listen
(C) listening
(D) listened

73. Mark and Hilary visit a new ______ country every year.

(A) foreign
(B) foreigner
(C) abroad
(D) out of

74. I ______ so thirsty! Let's go to the bar and have a drink.

(A) have
(B) do
(C) am
(D) will

75. They made part of the staff______ on Saturdays.

(A) work
(B) works
(C) working
(D) worked

76. He keeps ______ the same mistakes all the time.

(A) making
(B) doing
(C) to make
(D) to do

77. Put out your cigarette, sir. You ______ smoke here.

(A) have to
(B) must not
(C) need to
(D) are

78. When he finished ______, he invited the audience to ask questions.

(A) to speak
(B) speaking
(C) speaks
(D) speak

79. It is not worth ______ to convince them.

(A) trying
(B) to try
(C) try
(D) trial

80. If I ______ in the city, I would never drive to work.

(A) live
(B) lived
(C) living
(D) will live

PART V

Directions: The questions in this part of the test are based on reading materials such as notices, letters, forms, and advertisements. Choose the **one** word or phrase that best completes the sentence. Then mark your answer on your answer sheet.

Read the example:

NOTICE

CAFETERIA CLOSED

Will reopen Monday, June 5

What will happen on June 5?

(A) The workers have a day off.
(B) The cafeteria will open.
(C) The prices will go down.
(D) The school will close.

Sample Answer
(A) ● (C) (D)

The notice says that the cafeteria is closed and will open on June 5. Therefore, you should choose answer (B).

Now begin work on the questions.

Questions 81-83 refer to the following advertisement.

HOME SEARCH NEWSLETTER – *JUNE*

For rent

2-room apartment with separate kitchen on Spring Rose avenue
Refurbished and fully furnished (kingsize bed, couch, dishwasher, washing machine)
6th floor with elevator

Bright, clean and calm
Nice building and environment
Ideal for single or couple

900 dollars / month + 2-month deposit *(available September 30)*

Contact: Home Search Agency for details
(361) 761 2000　(Monday to Saturday 8:30am – 7:00pm)

81. What is said about the apartment?

(A) It has been renovated.
(B) There is no elevator.
(C) It is empty.
(D) There is not much light.

82. What kind of business is Home Search Agency?

(A) A travel agency.
(B) A car rental agency.
(C) A real estate agency.
(D) An advertising agency.

83. When will the apartment be free?

(A) This spring.
(B) In September.
(C) Immediately.
(D) On Monday.

Questions 84-86 refer to the following notice.

Brentwood Park Hotel

The Brentwood Park Hotel is a superior class hotel ideally located between the picturesque Old Town and the business district.
It offers various facilities that will make your stay in our city an unforgettable one…

3 restaurants

maid service

gift shop

business center with PC, fax machine, internet access, laptop and cell phone rentals

children's playground

fitness room

safety deposit boxes

conference center

Hotel regulations

- Pets not allowed.
- Bookings are subject to a 30-dollar fee for any cancelation or change less than 24 hours before arrival date.
- No refunds for early checkouts.

84. Who cannot stay at the hotel?

(A) Children.
(B) Maids.
(C) Animals.
(D) Businessmen.

85. In what case is there an additional charge?

(A) Early checkout.
(B) Last minute cancelation.
(C) To get a refund.
(D) To access the business center.

86. What can be done at the hotel?

(A) Presents can be bought.
(B) Tennis courts can be reserved.
(C) 30-dollar books can be bought.
(D) Cars can be rented.

Questions 87-89 refer to the following note.

NOTE

> In order to make your stay more enjoyable, we inform our guests that this elevator is being renovated until September 1 at 12:00pm.
> We are sorry for the inconvenience that may be caused.

87. Where would this notice most likely be seen?

(A) In the street.
(B) In a hotel.
(C) In a hospital.
(D) On a bus.

88. What will happen on September 1?

(A) The renovation period will continue.
(B) The renovation period will begin.
(C) The elevator will be replaced.
(D) The elevator will be back in service.

89. What is said about the current situation?

(A) It is very hopeless.
(B) It is very pleasant.
(C) It is temporary.
(D) It will never improve.

Questions 90-92 refer to the following e-mail message.

From: Steven Hunt <s.hunt@eurobooks.com>
To: <karen.brown@blt.eur.com>
Date: 10 March
Subject: next meeting

Following our phone conversation this morning, I would like to confirm our meeting on 16 March at 2:30 pm to discuss the new advertising campaign. I apologize for the change of plans and hope this does not cause any problems. A map showing how to get to our new office follows on the next page.

I look forward to seeing you.

Regards,

Steven

90. When did Steven call Karen?

(A) On March 16.
(B) At 2:30pm.
(C) Earlier today.
(D) Yesterday morning.

91. What is the subject of the meeting?

(A) A change of plans.
(B) An advertising campaign.
(C) A new office.
(D) A contract to sign.

92. What is said in this message?

(A) A map has been added to the message.
(B) Steven wants Karen to call him back.
(C) Steven wants to cancel the meeting.
(D) Steven wants to put off the meeting.

Questions 93-95 refer to the following invitation.

World-famous photographer Ethan ARMSTRONG has pleasure in inviting you to the opening reception of his gallery.

On Wednesday, June 10
from 6:00 to 8:00pm

The ARMSTRONG Gallery
7902 N. Pinebrook Drive
Beverly Hills, CA 90210

Some photographs from his new book "A Bird's Eye View" will be sold. Part of the proceeds from the sale will be donated to The Meredith Sullivan foundation for young contemporary artists.

93. Who sent this invitation?

(A) Some photographers.
(B) A painter.
(C) The Meredith Sullivan Foundation.
(D) Ethan Armstrong.

94. What will go to the Meredith Sullivan Foundation?

(A) Armstrong's new book.
(B) Some photographs.
(C) A percentage of the sale.
(D) All the proceeds from the sale.

95. What will happen during the reception?

(A) Photographs from the book will be given.
(B) Ethan Armstrong will receive a donation.
(C) Young artists will take photographs.
(D) Guests will be able to buy some pictures.

Questions 96-97 refer to the following chart.

STATISTICS

UK SALES OF MOBILE PHONES (THOUSANDS)
JULY- DECEMBER

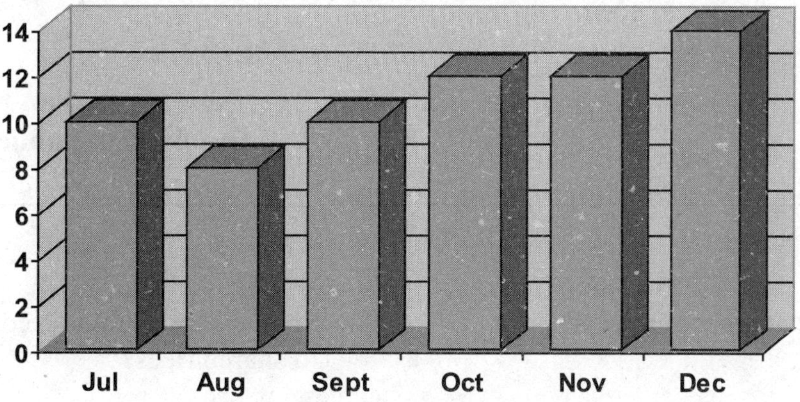

<u>NOTE</u>: *THIS CHART DOES NOT INCLUDE SALES OF MOBILE PHONES WITH BUILT-IN CAMERAS*

SOURCE: BSC DATA RESEARCH CENTRE

96. What does this bar chart tell us about sales of mobiles?

(A) Sales were higher in July than in September.
(B) Sales were the same in October and November.
(C) Sales decreased in September.
(D) Sales stayed at the same level in the last three months.

97. When did sales drop?

(A) In August.
(B) In September.
(C) In October.
(D) In December.

Questions 98-100 refer to the following extracts.

MILLIONS OF DOLLARS WORTH OF DAMAGE AFTER HURRICANE IN FLORIDA

Prime Minister resigns after bribe scandal

REDMAN CO SHARE PRICES SINK TO LOWEST LEVEL SINCE 2001

New regulations to ban smoking in public places

98. What are these extracts?

(A) Headlines.
(B) Articles.
(C) Questions.
(D) Advertisements.

99. What is happening to Redman Co share prices?

(A) They are staying at the same level.
(B) They are decreasing.
(C) They are increasing.
(D) They are rising.

100. One of the articles refers to:

(A) A politician quitting his job.
(B) An earthquake.
(C) A new cigarette brand.
(D) A trip to Florida.

This is the end of the Reading portion of the test.

模拟测试 2
答题卡

LISTENING COMPREHENSION SECTION

PART Ⅰ
Photographs

15 questions

1.	A	B	C	D
2.	A	B	C	D
3.	A	B	C	D
4.	A	B	C	D
5.	A	B	C	D
6.	A	B	C	D
7.	A	B	C	D
8.	A	B	C	D
9.	A	B	C	D
10.	A	B	C	D
11.	A	B	C	D
12.	A	B	C	D
13.	A	B	C	D
14.	A	B	C	D
15.	A	B	C	D

PART Ⅱ
Question – Response

20 questions

16.	A	B	C
17.	A	B	C
18.	A	B	C
19.	A	B	C
20.	A	B	C
21.	A	B	C
22.	A	B	C
23.	A	B	C
24.	A	B	C
25.	A	B	C
26.	A	B	C
27.	A	B	C
28.	A	B	C
29.	A	B	C
30.	A	B	C
31.	A	B	C
32.	A	B	C
33.	A	B	C
34.	A	B	C
35.	A	B	C

PART Ⅲ
Short Conversations
and Short Talks

15 questions

36.	A	B	C	D
37.	A	B	C	D
38.	A	B	C	D
39.	A	B	C	D
40.	A	B	C	D
41.	A	B	C	D
42.	A	B	C	D
43.	A	B	C	D
44.	A	B	C	D
45.	A	B	C	D
46.	A	B	C	D
47.	A	B	C	D
48.	A	B	C	D
49.	A	B	C	D
50.	A	B	C	D

READING SECTION

PART Ⅳ
Incomplete Sentences

30 questions

51.	A	B	C	D
52.	A	B	C	D
53.	A	B	C	D
54.	A	B	C	D
55.	A	B	C	D
56.	A	B	C	D
57.	A	B	C	D
58.	A	B	C	D
59.	A	B	C	D
60.	A	B	C	D
61.	A	B	C	D
62.	A	B	C	D
63.	A	B	C	D
64.	A	B	C	D
65.	A	B	C	D

66.	A	B	C	D
67.	A	B	C	D
68.	A	B	C	D
69.	A	B	C	D
70.	A	B	C	D
71.	A	B	C	D
72.	A	B	C	D
73.	A	B	C	D
74.	A	B	C	D
75.	A	B	C	D
76.	A	B	C	D
77.	A	B	C	D
78.	A	B	C	D
79.	A	B	C	D
80.	A	B	C	D

PART Ⅴ
Reading Comprehension

20 questions

81.	A	B	C	D
82.	A	B	C	D
83.	A	B	C	D
84.	A	B	C	D
85.	A	B	C	D
86.	A	B	C	D
87.	A	B	C	D
88.	A	B	C	D
89.	A	B	C	D
90.	A	B	C	D
91.	A	B	C	D
92.	A	B	C	D
93.	A	B	C	D
94.	A	B	C	D
95.	A	B	C	D
96.	A	B	C	D
97.	A	B	C	D
98.	A	B	C	D
99.	A	B	C	D
100.	A	B	C	D

托业桥 Practice Test 2

LISTENING COMPREHENSION

This is the listening section of the test. There are three parts to this section.

PART Ⅰ

Directions: You will see a picture in your test book and you will hear four short statements.

Look at the picture in your test book and choose the statement that best describes what you see in the picture. Then mark your answer on your answer sheet.

Look at the sample below and listen to the four statements.

Statement (B), "The boys are reading", best describes what you see in the picture. Therefore, you should choose answer (B).

Sample Answer

(A) ● (C) (D)

Now let us begin Part Ⅰ with question number one.

1.

2.

3.

Source: www.bigfoto.com

4.

5.

6.

7.

8.

9.

10.

11.

12.

13.

14.

15.

PART Ⅱ 

Directions: Now, you will hear a question or statement followed by three responses. Choose the best response to each question or statement.

Now listen to a sample question.

You will hear: Good morning, John. How are you?

You will also hear:
(A) I am fine, thank you.
(B) I am in the living room.
(C) My name is John.

Sample Answer
● (B) (C)

The best response to the question "How are you?" is choice (A), "I am fine, thank you." Therefore, you should choose answer (A).

Now let us begin Part Ⅱ with question number 16.

16. Mark your answer on your answer sheet.

17. Mark your answer on your answer sheet.

18. Mark your answer on your answer sheet.

19. Mark your answer on your answer sheet.

20. Mark your answer on your answer sheet.

21. Mark your answer on your answer sheet.

22. Mark your answer on your answer sheet.

23. Mark your answer on your answer sheet.

24. Mark your answer on your answer sheet.

25. Mark your answer on your answer sheet.

26. Mark your answer on your answer sheet.

27. Mark your answer on your answer sheet.

28. Mark your answer on your answer sheet.

29. Mark your answer on your answer sheet.

30. Mark your answer on your answer sheet.

31. Mark your answer on your answer sheet.

32. Mark your answer on your answer sheet.

33. Mark your answer on your answer sheet.

34. Mark your answer on your answer sheet.

35. Mark your answer on your answer sheet.

PART Ⅲ

Directions: Now, you will hear several short talks or conversations.

In your test book, you will read a question followed by four answers. Choose the best answer to each question and mark it on your answer sheet.

Now let us begin Part III with question number 36.

36. What did the announcer say?

(A) It will be wet and windy.
(B) It was less cold yesterday.
(C) It will rain all day.
(D) It may snow.

37. Where are the speakers?

(A) In a doctor's surgery.
(B) In a shop.
(C) In a pharmacy.
(D) In a restaurant.

38. When will the plane arrive in New York?

(A) On time.
(B) In a few minutes.
(C) 2 hours late.
(D) In 3 hours.

39. Why can't the man speak to Ms Bates?

(A) He can't leave a message.
(B) Her line is busy.
(C) He's got the wrong number.
(D) She's out of town.

40. What does the woman want to do?

(A) Get some cash.
(B) Pay by check.
(C) Report a lost driver's license.
(D) Get a new passport.

41. What is Alex Campbell's profession?

(A) Journalist.
(B) Photographer.
(C) Travel agent.
(D) Businessman.

42. What does the man want to do?

(A) Get his money back.
(B) Buy a camera.
(C) Sell a camera.
(D) Return to work.

43. Where does this conversation take place?

(A) In a swimming pool.
(B) In a department store.
(C) In a bank.
(D) In a restaurant.

44. Where is this announcement heard?

(A) In a restaurant.
(B) In a hospital.
(C) At a bus station.
(D) At an airport.

45. What is the man's problem?

(A) He has lost the brochure.
(B) He lives in Cyprus.
(C) He left yesterday.
(D) He can't find his desk.

46. What does Mr Miller want to do?

(A) Order a product.
(B) Deliver a product.
(C) Cancel his order.
(D) Find out about his order.

47. What is the speaker going to do?

(A) Present production figures.
(B) Ask questions.
(C) Present a new product.
(D) Give a brief talk.

48. What does the woman want to do?

(A) Reserve a table.
(B) Put a book on the table.
(C) Cancel a reservation.
(D) Go to the restaurant on Friday.

49. Where is the post office?

(A) In the travel agency.
(B) In the department store.
(C) On Hudson Lane.
(D) In the mall.

50. When is the business center closed?

(A) On Thursdays.
(B) On Fridays.
(C) At 7:30am.
(D) At 9:40pm.

This is the end of the Listening Comprehension portion of the test. Turn to Part Ⅳ of the test.

YOU WILL HAVE THIRTY-FIVE MINUTES TO COMPLETE PARTS Ⅳ AND Ⅴ OF THE TEST.

READING

This is the reading section of the test. There are two parts to this section.

PART Ⅳ

Directions: This part of the test has incomplete sentences. There are four words or phrases, marked (A), (B), (C), and (D), under each sentence. Choose the **one** word or phrase that best completes the sentence. Then mark your answer on your answer sheet.

Example:

Please turn off your computer at the _____ of the day.

(A) ends
(B) ending
(C) end
(D) ended

Sample Answer
(A) (B) ● (D)

The sentence should read, "Please turn off your computer at the end of the day." Therefore, you should choose answer (C).

Now begin work on the questions.

51. Ms Alexander expected her students _____ on time.

(A) arrive
(B) to arrive
(C) arriving
(D) arrived

52. How many dogs and cats _____?

(A) you have
(B) are you having
(C) do you have
(D) will you

53. I _____ to Austria two weeks ago.

(A) went
(B) have gone
(C) have been
(D) go

54. Do I _____ to fill out this form now?

(A) must
(B) have
(C) should
(D) will

55. They agreed _____ 3,000 units per month.

(A) buy
(B) to buy
(C) buying
(D) buyer

56. _____ that it will probably rain during the night.

(A) I think
(B) I am thinking
(C) Thinks
(D) Thinking

57. Some people _____ using public transport to go to work.

(A) likes
(B) like to
(C) like
(D) they like

58. Who is in charge _____ after sales service?

(A) of
(B) for
(C) with
(D) to

59. I will show you the right way _____ do it.

(A) of
(B) to
(C) for
(D) through

60. Homemade food is ______ frozen food.

(A) different of
(B) different from
(C) same as
(D) the same

61. They made some new business contacts _____ their trip to Brazil.

(A) during
(B) when
(C) while
(D) as soon as

62. Next time I will take you to the _____ restaurant in town.

(A) cheaply
(B) cheaper
(C) cheapest
(D) less cheap

63. The train has not left the station ______.

(A) never
(B) still
(C) always
(D) yet

64. Why do I always _____ the same mistakes?

(A) do
(B) make
(C) take
(D) speak

65. His friends _____ him to be very careful.

(A) advised
(B) suggested
(C) said
(D) explained

66. Did you _____ to your parents yesterday?

(A) phone
(B) tell
(C) call
(D) talk

67. He works for the same company _____ me.

(A) than
(B) that
(C) as
(D) like

68. She invited her parents and her best friends _____.

(A) too
(B) also
(C) either
(D) both

69. Does she _____ work on Sundays?

(A) every week
(B) once a week
(C) as well
(D) always

70. Neither Antonio _____ an invitation to the wedding.

(A) nor Angela received
(B) nor Angela didn't receive
(C) and Angela receive
(D) either Angela did receive

71. I _____ this company six months ago.

(A) joined
(B) am joining
(C) join
(D) joins

72. Do her parents let her _____ TV?

(A) to watch
(B) watch
(C) watching
(D) that she watches

73. He made me _____ when he said he had lost his shoe.

(A) laugh
(B) to laugh
(C) laughing
(D) laughter

74. A tourist asked me _____ directions to go the museum.

(A) for
(B) to
(C) of
(D) at

75. Thank you very much _____ your help.

(A) for
(B) of
(C) with
(D) about

76. I will talk to him on _____.

(A) June
(B) next Monday
(C) Monday
(D) tomorrow

77. He is not very pleased _____ his test scores.

(A) of
(B) to
(C) at
(D) with

78. The agreement between the two countries will not be announced _____ the election.

(A) until
(B) as soon as
(C) while
(D) yet

79. Both Sam _____ Rachel called her for Christmas.

(A) or
(B) and
(C) either
(D) but

80. Her test scores are much better this year. She has _____ a lot of progress.

(A) made
(B) done
(C) taken
(D) been

PART V

Directions: The questions in this part of the test are based on reading materials such as notices, letters, forms, and advertisements. Choose the **one** word or phrase that best completes the sentence. Then mark your answer on your answer sheet.

Read the example:

NOTICE

CAFETERIA CLOSED

Will reopen Monday, June 5

What will happen on June 5?
(A) The workers have a day off.
(B) The cafeteria will open.
(C) The prices will go down.
(D) The school will close.

Sample Answer
(A) ● (C) (D)

The notice says that the cafeteria is closed and will open on June 5. Therefore, you should choose answer (B).

Now begin work on the questions.

Questions 81-83 refer to the following message.

Hi Justin,

How are you? I'm so glad you can make it to my birthday party next Saturday. I'll show you round my new house. Here's how to get there from the train station. It's about a 10-minute walk.

Walk out of the station and take the first street on the right. Carry straight on for about 200 yards and take the second on the right. Go straight on, past Memorial Church. Cross the bridge, and at the traffic-lights turn right into Lincoln Street. Go through the park, and turn right. My house is on the corner of Oakridge Street and River Road, next to the public library.
Call me if you have any trouble finding the house or shall I ask my brother to pick you up at the station?

Megan

81. What is the purpose of the message?

(A) To invite Justin to a party.
(B) To buy a new house.
(C) To explain the way from the station.
(D) To cancel a party.

82. Where does Megan live?

(A) Close to a library.
(B) Near a bookstore.
(C) Opposite a river.
(D) In Lincoln Street.

83. What is Justin supposed to do?

(A) Turn right out of the station.
(B) Go through Memorial Church.
(C) Pick up Megan's brother.
(D) Go under the bridge.

Questions 84-86 refer to the following article.

Modern Traveler ***magazine***

Traveling long distances by air and crossing time zones in a flash is exciting but can also be stressful and very disturbing for your biological clock.

This month, **Modern Traveler** *magazine* gives you ***5*** easy tips to make your next air travel experience a pleasant one.

- Plan your trip in advance to avoid last minute stress.
- Get a good night's sleep just prior to departure.
- Don't eat rich or fatty foods.
- Drink mineral water instead of coffee or tea.
- Get as much exercise as you can before and during the flight: walking and stretching exercises in your seat all help to get rid of stress.

84. What is the main purpose of this article?
(A) To advertise a brand of mineral water.
(B) To announce a discount on airline tickets.
(C) To cancel a flight.
(D) To inform passengers.

85. What is recommended?
(A) Drinking coffee.
(B) Drinking tea.
(C) Sleeping well before the flight.
(D) Wearing comfortable clothes.

86. What is said in this article?
(A) It is better to plan one's trips at the last minute.
(B) Traveling by boat is exciting.
(C) Exercising can help fight against stress.
(D) Traveling frequently is dangerous.

Questions 87-89 refer to the following schedule.

NEWSLINE fm 95

You'll be the first to know

Friday December 21

6:00	***Newsline Evening Report***	A complete round up of the latest news.
6:30	***Newsline Business Update***	Special reports from our experts in international economics and all the latest financial and business news (daily).
7:00	***Eye on Hi-Tech***	Nothing but simple terms to tell you what you need to know to understand all the new technologies (Fridays).
8:00	***Newsline Evening Report***	A complete round up of the latest news.
8:30	***Science Today***	This quarterly program explores big scientific issues of today's world and the impact they may have on our lives tomorrow.
9:30	***Insights 2000***	A complete analysis of the current political trends and issues (Tuesdays and Fridays).

87. Which program is shown every three months?

(A) *Science Today.*
(B) *Newsline Business Update.*
(C) *Insights 2000.*
(D) *Eye On Hi-Tech.*

88. What is *Insights 2000* about?

(A) Sports.
(B) Politics.
(C) Business.
(D) Environment.

89. How often is *Eye on Hi-Tech* scheduled?

(A) Every day.
(B) Every two weeks.
(C) Once a week.
(D) Twice a week.

Questions 90-92 refer to the following notice.

Celebrated Australian novelist Norman WATTS
winner of the University Press prize
will discuss and sign his latest work
"Murder at the Opera"
Tuesday September 28
5:30 – 7:30
at the new Metropolitan Center
Call (510) 518 7000 for more information.

90. Who is Norman Watts?

(A) A student.
(B) A university professor.
(C) A journalist.
(D) A writer.

91. What is the announcement about?

(A) A literary discussion.
(B) The opening of a new center.
(C) An award ceremony.
(D) A cocktail party.

92. What is NOT said in this announcement?

(A) The event will last two hours.
(B) Tickets can be reserved by phone.
(C) The novelist will talk about his book.
(D) Norman Watts is famous.

Questions 93-95 refer to the following advertisement.

Say goodbye to your paper organizer…!!!

Discover the new **Orion SL-300*i***

The revolutionary digital organizer that will change your life

- organize appointments in a few seconds
- store hundreds of names and addresses, photographs
- access all your personal notes easily
- take your important files with you to meetings or on the road
- set alarms and reminders
- share information with your desktop computer

Orion SL-300*i* can do it all. And so much more…

Buy your Orion SL-300***i*** now and get a free memory expansion card to store all your data.*

**This special offer expires March 26.*

93. What is the Orion SL-300***i***?

(A) An electronic organizer.

(B) A paper date book.

(C) A camera.

(D) A desktop computer.

94. What can you get if you buy an Orion SL-300***i*** now?

(A) A 10% discount.

(B) An expensive card.

(C) A memory card.

(D) An alarm clock.

95. What does the Orion SL-300***i*** allow users to do?

(A) Fill out important forms.

(B) Play video games.

(C) Connect to the Internet.

(D) Exchange data with a computer.

Questions 96-97 refer to the following chart.

The following chart shows the most frequently watched television program types over the last three years.

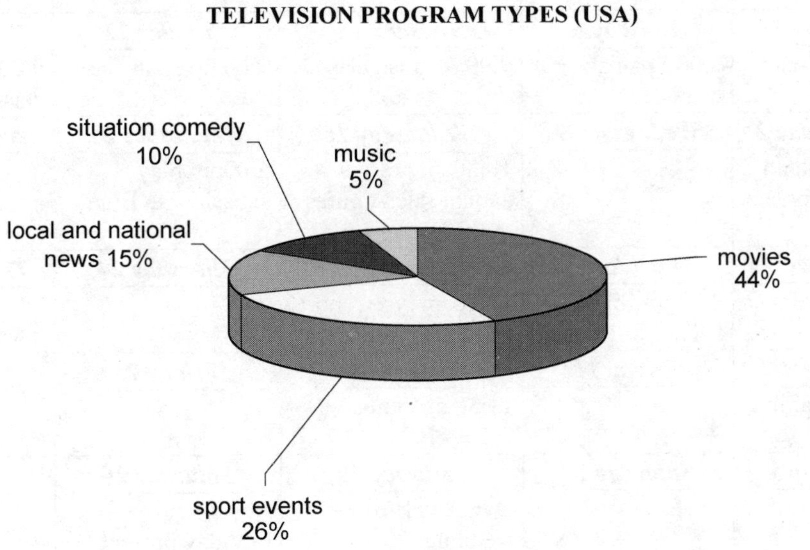

Figure 1

Source: Sedgwick Global Surveys Inc.

96. What information does this pie chart provide us with?

(A) Figures concerning next year.
(B) Figures covering a three-year period.
(C) The percentage of people watching programs for children.
(D) Detailed figures for each city.

97. What is the least frequently watched type of television program?

(A) Local and national news.
(B) Music.
(C) Sports events.
(D) Movies.

Questions 98-100 refer to the following page from a calendar.

JUNE

	Monday 7	***Monday 14***	***Monday 21***	***Monday 28***
Tuesday 1 12:00pm lunch with Sam	***Tuesday 8*** 9:00 Spanish class	***Tuesday 15*** 9:00 Spanish class	***Tuesday 22*** 9:00 Spanish class	***Tuesday 29*** 9:00 Spanish class
Wednesday 2 4:30pm attend sales conference	***Wednesday 9***	***Wednesday 16*** 10:30am present annual sales figures to the board	***Wednesday 23*** 5:00pm play squash with Brad	***Wednesday 30***
Thursday 3 2:00pm training session 1	***Thursday 10*** 2:30pm flight BS217 to Boston	***Thursday 17*** 10:00am type report about trip to Boston	***Thursday 24***	***Thursday 31*** 7:00pm radio interview
Friday 4 2:00pm training session 2	***Friday 11***	***Friday 18*** 11:30am dentist	***Friday 25***	
Saturday 5 Shopping	***Saturday 12***	***Saturday 19*** Dylan and Amy's wedding	***Saturday 26*** Buy Terry's birthday present	
Sunday 6 Barbecue party	***Sunday 13*** Fishing with Dad	***Sunday 20***	***Sunday 27*** Terry's birthday party	

98. What is **NOT** scheduled for the third week of the month?
(A) A trip.
(B) A presentation.
(C) A medical appointment.
(D) A language class.

99. What is planned on a Thursday morning?
(A) A trip to Boston.
(B) A report to write.
(C) A training session.
(D) A radio interview.

100. What is happening on a Saturday?
(A) Terry is buying a birthday present.
(B) Terry is making a presentation.
(C) Dylan and Amy are moving to a new house.
(D) Dylan and Amy are getting married.

This is the end of the Reading portion of the test.

附录 A

练习题
听力文本与答案

第3章

Exercise 1

参考答案

What can you see in the picture?
A part of the building is covered by scaffolding.
The building is being renovated.
The windows are closed.

Where was the picture taken?
They are outdoors.
They are near a building.

Exercise 2

Some people are going up the stairs.

第4章

Exercise 1

参考答案

1. When was your daughter born?
   When did you go to Korea?

2. Would you like a cup of tea?
   Do you want a glass of water?

3. Where are you staying?
   Where was the convention held?

4. How long are you going to stay?
   How long can I keep the books I borrowed?

5. What was the weather like?

6. Was it your first visit there?

7. Why are you so late?

8. Whose car is this?
Is this your suitcase?

Exercise 2

1.	Who's going to pick you up at the station?	My husband.
2.	When was Maria's brother born?	In 1975.
3.	Why didn't you attend the Spanish class this morning?	I woke up too late.
4.	Shall I get you something to drink?	A cup of coffee, please.
5.	The football game is on Saturday, isn't it?	No, it's on Tuesday.
6.	Would you like to go to the beach with us?	Sorry, but I have to go downtown.
7.	You're not going to tell him, are you?	I'm afraid I'll have to.
8.	Can I borrow your stapler?	I've already lent it to Barbara.
9.	That's the Eiffel Tower, isn't it?	That's right.

第5章

Exercise 1

听力文本

Ladies and gentlemen, it is my pleasure to introduce to you the Olympic Medallist Tatiana Vassileva. A native of Saint-Petersburg, Ms Vassileva began her swimming career at the age of fourteen and won her first medal in Australia two years later. She is in our studio in New York today to present the book she has written about her childhood and her projects for the future.

女士们先生们，很荣幸地向大家介绍奥林匹克奖牌得主塔提安娜・瓦西列

娃女士。她来自圣彼得堡，从14岁开始从事游泳并在2年后在澳大利亚获得了她职业生涯中的第一块奖牌。今天，她来到了我们位于纽约的演播室，并带来她自己写的一本书，内容是关于她的童年及未来规划的。

1.	Who is probably speaking?	**D.**	An interviewer.
2.	Where does this talk take place?	**J.**	In New York.
3.	Who is Ms Vassileva?	**A.**	A swimmer.
4.	What is the book about?	**C.**	Her childhood.
5.	When did she win her first medal?	**G.**	At the age of sixteen.

Exercise 2

听力文本

Woman:	How much is the fare to go downtown?
Man:	About eight dollars. And it takes thirty minutes to get there.
Woman:	Ok. Can you take me to the Museum of Modern Art on Baker Street, please?
女士：到市中心要多少钱？	
男士：大概 8 美元。到那里需要 30 分钟。	
女士：好的。请拉我去贝克尔街的现代艺术博物馆好吗？	

1. How long does it take to go downtown? (C) Half an hour.

2. How much is the fare? (B) About eight dollars.

3. What does the woman want to know? (B) The fare.

4. Who is the woman probably speaking to? (B) A taxi driver.

5. Where does she want to go? (A) To the Museum.

6. What is said in this conversation? (A) The Museum is located downtown.

第 7 章

Exercise 1

UNDERESTIMATE
INTERVIEWEE
STEWARDESS
SUCCESSFUL
INTERDEPENDENT
DISAPPEAR
HEROISM
JAPANESE
WORTHLESS
CARELESSNESS
INHOSPITABLE
UNDERGROUND
IMPOSSIBLE
STRENGTHEN

Exercise 2

1 Why didn't you **ATTEND** the **LECTURE** on German literature?

2 Employees usually have lunch at the **CANTEEN** between 12:00 and 1:00.

3 Do you **REALIZE** this is the fifth time you have been late?

4 The shop **DECEIVED** customers by selling second hand books as new ones.

5 The most **SENSIBLE** thing to do would be to ask the receptionist.

6 The Congressman is very **SENSITIVE** to the problems of homeless people.

7 The **FABRIC** they used to make the bride's dress was bought in Italy.

8 I borrowed this book about Italian art from the public **LIBRARY**.

9 I studied medieval **HISTORY** at college.

10 After a series of difficult negotiations, he **EVENTUALLY** agreed to sign the contract.

Exercise 3

1. The *price* of cars has increased by 2% since the beginning of the year.
2. Everybody attended the meeting *except* the manager.
3. She is not very *interested* in baseball.

4. The government's *economic* policy led to a major crisis.
5. They were deeply *affected* by the news.
6. He was so *bored* with the movie that he left before the end.
7. Why did you park your *car* there?
8. *Wash* your hands and brush your teeth.
9. I'm trying to lose some *weight*.
10. I have already made *plans* for the weekend.
11. Hurry up! I don't want to arrive *late*.
12. I don't know what to *wear* for the party.
13. I'm not tall enough to *reach* the books which are on the shelf.
14. I *read* a novel by Charles Dickens last summer.

第8章

Exercise 1

- Where does Satoshi sell its products? Holland.
- How many people does Satoshi employ? 125,000.
- What does Klemp produce? Food for animals.

Exercise 2

Keep - To continue doing something, or to do it repeatedly.

Train - A group of carriages connected together and pulled by a railway engine to carry people or goods.

Catch - To get on a train, bus or aircraft in order to travel to a destination.

Bear - To accept, tolerate, or endure something/someone unpleasant.

Wind - A current of air moving across the earth's surface.

Reception - Place in a hotel or office building where people go when they first arrive.

Kind - Sort, type.

Exercise 3

This document is a greetings card.	FALSE
You must send an e-mail to get details about the products.	FALSE
Customers cannot change their profiles.	FALSE
Customers have to send an e-mail to unsubscribe from the newsletter.	TRUE
Customers have to call 0800 525 028 to stop receiving special offers.	FALSE
By clicking on the link, customers can get more information.	TRUE
This offer is sent to all customers.	FALSE
Products can be purchased by sending a fax.	TRUE

Exercise 4

What kind of document is this?	*An advertisement.*
What is mentioned?	*Ceiling tiles.*
What do you get if you call?	*An evaluation of the cost.*

第 10 章

Exercise 1

1. (D) lease
2. (A) furniture
3. (C) rented
4. (B) cellar
5. (B) railing
6. (B) roof
7. (B) crane
8. (A) move into
9. (C) pipes

10. (B) kitchen

Exercise 2

Railway

Exercise 3

1. (A) married
2. (D) outgoing
3. (B) elderly
4. (C) expecting
5. (B) pets
6. (C) held
7. (C) brought up
8. (B) deceiving
9. (C) make
10. (D) split up

Exercise 4

VERB	NOUN
Bring up	Upbringing
Educate	Education
Inherit	Inheritance
Marry, get married	Marriage
Be born	Birth
Get engaged	Engagement
Live	Life
Get divorced, divorce	Divorce
Adopt	Adoption

Exercise 5

1. (B) broke
2. (A) from
3. (C) disease
4. (D) recovering
5. (C) on weight
6. (D) caught
7. (A) prescribed
8. (D) coughing

9. (A) injured
10. (A) harmful

Exercise 6

Feather

Exercise 7

NOUN	ADJECTIVE
Health	Healthy
Weakness	Weak
Pain	Painful, painless
Illness	Ill
Harm	Harmful, harmless
Surgery, surgeon	Surgical
Contagion	Contagious
Sickness	Sick
Pregnancy	Pregnant
Fitness	Fit

Exercise 8

1. (B) looking forward to
2. (A) boring
3. (B) proud
4. (B) with
5. (B) dared
6. (B) would rather
7. (B) afraid
8. (B) disappointed
9. (A) in the mood for
10. (B) advised

Exercise 9

1	Accept	***F***	Refuse
2	Amuse	***G***	Bore
3	Awful	***I***	Pleasant
4	Desperate	***H***	Hopeful
5	Dull	***A***	Interesting

6	Enjoy	*D*	Hate
7	Generous	*E*	Mean
8	Intelligent	*B*	Silly
9	Praise	*C*	Blame

Exercise 10

1. (C) attend
2. (C) learn
3. (B) dropped out
4. (B) graduated
5. (C) course
6. (A) pass
7. (B) compulsory
8. (D) homework
9. (A) scholarship
10. (B) knowledge

Exercise 11

Housework

Exercise 12

NOUN	ADJECTIVE
Friend	Friendly
Interest	Interesting
Theory	Theoretical
Literature	Literary
Knowledge	Knowledgeable
Proficiency	Proficient
Grammar	Grammatical
Education, educator	Educational
Philosophy	Philosophical

Exercise 13

1. (B) entrance

2.	(A)	loudly
3.	(A)	clips
4.	(D)	drawer
5.	(C)	file
6.	(C)	back
7.	(A)	order
8.	(A)	make
9.	(B)	printer
10.	(B)	seat

Exercise 14

Stove

Exercise 15

1	Pick up	***C***	Hang up
2	Plan	***D***	Cancel
3	Send	***B***	Receive
4	Recipient	***A***	Sender

Exercise 16

1.	(B)	cabinets
2.	(C)	rose
3.	(B)	an appointment
4.	(D)	subsidiaries
5.	(B)	manufacture
6.	(C)	leave
7.	(D)	turnover
8.	(C)	updated
9.	(B)	take place
10.	(B)	advice

Exercise 17

1	Add	***C***	Subtract
2	Borrow	***I***	Lend
3	Powerful	***F***	Weak
4	Increase	***H***	Fall
		B	Lower

5	Raise	*H*	Fall
		B	Lower
6	Poverty	*G*	Wealth
7	Cheap	*A*	Expensive
8	Buy	*D*	Sell
9	Profit	*E*	Loss
10	Earn	*J*	Lose

Exercise 18

VERB	NOUN
Apply	Application
Employ	Employment
Retire	Retirement
Recruit	Recruitment
Appoint	Appointment
Succeed	Success
Found	Foundation
Structure, restructure	Structure
Appraise	Appraisal
Promote	Promotion
Resign	Resignation
Advertise	Advertisement

Exercise 19

1. (B) left
2. (A) performed
3. (B) subtitled
4. (C) beat
5. (D) on stage
6. (C) locker room
7. (B) seats
8. (B) role
9. (D) show
10. (B) playwrights

Exercise 20

VERB	NOUN
Exhibit	Exhibit, exhibition, exhibitor
Produce	Producer
Direct	Direction, director
Paint	Painting
Sing	Singer, song
Create	Creation
Write	Writer, writing
Run	Runner
Act	Actor, actress, action

Exercise 21

1. (B) waitress
2. (B) meal
3. (B) overdone
4. (A) book
5. (C) on
6. (C) order
7. (B) dishes
8. (B) tip
9. (B) have
10. (A) bill

Exercise 22

Desert

Exercise 23

1. (C) close
2. (B) out of stock
3. (C) expensive
4. (D) accept
5. (C) pay
6. (A) currency
7. (B) elevator

8. (B) charge
9. (C) stamp
10. (A) size

Exercise 24

1. She bought several expensive *items* at the new department store.
2. As she is a good customer, the salesman gave her a 5% *discount.*
3. She *borrowed* money from her best friends to pay for her apartment.
4. The fresh food department is in the *basement.*
5. This dress is too expensive. I can't *afford* it.
6. How much is this suit? I can't find the price *tag.*
7. This shop sells antique furniture at *bargain prices.*
8. Some people spend more *money* on their cars than on their food.
9. As the blouse was not my size, I returned it to the shop and asked for a *refund.*
10. Can you *deliver* two pizzas to my apartment in ten minutes?

Exercise 25

1. They're going to open a new store in Riverdale.
2. I'd like to buy a sweater for my son.
3. How much does this scarf cost?
4. Do you accept credit cards?
5. The clerk forgot to give me a receipt.
6. Can I be of any assistance, Sir?

Exercise 26

1. (A) on
2. (C) check
3. (C) heavy
4. (D) valid
5. (D) platform
6. (C) miss
7. (B) cancel
8. (C) one-way
9. (A) is
10. (D) delayed

Exercise 27

1	Land	***D***	Take off
2	Early	***I***	Late
3	Board	***E***	Get off
4	Outskirts	***F***	Center
5	Guest	***H***	Host
6	Arrival	***G***	Departure
7	Occupied	***B***	Vacant
8	Heavy	***A***	Light
9	Catch	***C***	Miss

Exercise 28

1. (B) correspondent
2. (A) issued
3. (D) polls
4. (B) cloudy
5. (C) headlines
6. (A) announced
7. (D) scored
8. (B) whether
9. (A) newspaper
10. (C) subscribed

Exercise 29

1	Cloudy	***C***	Sunny
2	Freeze	***E***	Melt
3	Supporter	***G***	Opponent
4	Deny	***A***	Admit
5	Defeat	***I***	Victory
6	Trust	***H***	Suspect

7	Reply	***B***	Question
8	Major	***D***	Minor
9	Guilty	***F***	Innocent

Exercise 30

Dishwasher

第11章

Exercise 1

1. (A) rains
2. (B) usually attends
3. (A) am taking
4. (B) want
5. (A) flows
6. (B) is staying
7. (B) is still playing
8. (A) do
9. (A) usually
10. (C) this week

Exercise 2

1. (A) found
2. (C) I have ever seen
3. (A) has ever been
4. (B) hasn't sent
5. (A) have you known
6. (A) did they have
7. (B) has sold
8. (B) broke down
9. (A) did you meet

10. (B) How long

Exercise 3

1. (B) was taken
2. (A) has ridden
3. (A) told
4. (B) had spoken
5. (B) had you been living
6. (C) had already left
7. (A) has gone
8. (B) since
9. (B) had never flown
10. (B) he had been working

Exercise 4

1. (A) will help
2. (B) are you doing
3. (A) I am going to buy
4. (C) will be
5. (B) as soon as
6. (B) I am
7. (B) you want
8. (D) leaves
9. (A) am playing
10. (A) have

Exercise 5

1. (B) don't call
2. (B) would get
3. (A) had lost
4. (A) had told
5. (B) wouldn't
6. (B) would call
7. (A) would you have done
8. (A) would happen

9. (B) would
10. (B) would like to

Exercise 6

1. (C) typing
2. (B) taking
3. (B) to buy
4. (A) to go
5. (C) locking
6. (B) to be
7. (B) to wait
8. (C) taking
9. (B) to invite
10. (D) stealing

Exercise 7

1	With	*F*	Without
2	From	*A*	To
3	In (to)	*H*	Out (of)
4	On	*C*	Off
5	Down	*E*	Up
6	Above	*I*	Below
7	Against	*G*	For
8	After	*B*	Before
9	Behind	*D*	In front of

Exercise 8

1. (D) with
2. (B) of selling
3. (A) in solving
4. (B) for
5. (D) of
6. (A) in

7. (B) with
8. (D) on
9. (C) from
10. (B) from

Exercise 9

1. (A) an
2. (C) a
3. (B) the
4. (B) a week
5. (A) breakfast
6. (C) to
7. (A) some information
8. (D) a seven-hour
9. (A) The French
10. (A) the poor

Exercise 10

1. (A) his
2. (C) each other
3. (D) of yours
4. (A) I
5. (B) himself
6. (B) yourself
7. (B) me
8. (B) yourself
9. (C) itself
10. (A) one another

Exercise 11

1. (A) as easy as
2. (C) the most expensive
3. (A) better
4. (A) the worst

5. (C) than
6. (B) further
7. (C) worse
8. (C) as
9. (A) quicker
10. (B) most

Exercise 12

1	Older	***J***	Younger
2	Uglier	***G***	More beautiful
3	Farther	***I***	Closer
4	Cheaper	***D***	More expensive
5	Bigger	***B***	Smaller
6	Easier	***H***	More difficult
7	Better	***A***	Worse
8	Cleaner	***E***	Dirtier
9	Taller	***C***	Shorter
10	Colder	***F***	Warmer

Exercise 13

1. (C) unless
2. (B) provided
3. (B) although
4. (D) whether
5. (A) of them
6. (B) until
7. (C) previously
8. (B) In the end
9. (A) between
10. (B) in order to

附录 B

小测试及模拟测试听力文本与答案

小测试 1 — 听力文本

1.

(A) The dog is running.
(B) The man is working.
(C) The man is walking his dog.
(D) The man is feeding the dog.

（A）那只小狗在跑。
（B）那个男人在工作。
（C）那个男人在遛狗。
（D）那个男人在喂狗。

2.

(A) A man is reading a paper.
(B) The man is writing a paper.
(C) The man is sitting on a train.
(D) There are two people on the bench.

（A）一个男人在读一份报纸。
（B）那个男人正在写论文。
（C）那个男人正坐在火车上。
（D）长椅上坐着两个人。

3.

(A) The men are loading the truck.
(B) The men are carrying large boxes.
(C) A man is climbing into the truck.
(D) Crates are stacked outside the truck.

（A）那些男人正在往卡车上装货物。
（B）那些男人正在搬运大箱子。
（C）一个男人正爬进卡车。
（D）板条箱被堆在卡车外面。

4.

(A) The crowd is listening to a concert.
(B) The concert has just ended.
(C) The people are waiting for the bus.
(D) There isn't anybody on the stage.

（A）观众正在听音乐会。
（B）音乐会刚刚结束。
（C）人们正在等待公交车。
（D）舞台上什么人都没有。

5.

(A) The children are reading.
(B) The woman is holding a shopping bag.
(C) The children are riding horses.
(D) The woman is looking at the child.

（A）孩子们正在阅读。
（B）那个女人正拿着一个购物袋。
（C）孩子们正在骑马。
（D）那个女人正看着那个孩子。

6. (Woman) How often do you play tennis?
(Man) (A) With my new racket.
(B) At the club.
(C) Once a week.

（女）　你多久玩一次网球？

（男）　（A）用我的新球拍。
（B）在俱乐部。
（C）一周一次。

7.　(Woman)　How long have you been living in Hong Kong?
(Man)　(A) Five miles long.
(B) 20 years ago.
(C) For twenty years.

（女）　你在香港住了多久？

（男）　（A）五英里长。
（B）20 年前。
（C）20 年了。

8.　(Man 1)　Where does the meeting take place?
(Man 2)　(A) At 2:00pm.
(B) In room C12.
(C) To review the sales results.

（男 1）　会议在哪里召开？

（男 2）　（A）下午两点。
（B）在 C12 房间。
（C）检查销售结果。

9.　(Man)　Do you know Claudia?
(Woman)　(A) Yes, I know.
(B) No, I'm not.
(C) Yes, I do.

（男）　你认识克罗蒂亚吗？
（女）　（A）是的，我知道。
（B）不，我不是。
（C）是的，我认识。

10. (Woman 1) Have you been waiting long?
(Woman 2) (A) Just a few minutes.
(B) 6 miles long.
(C) In the convention hall.

（女 1）　你等了很久吗？
（女 2）　（A）只有几分钟。
（B）6 英里长。
（C）在大会堂。

11. (Man) Can I have extension 470, please?
(Woman) (A) Until 4:17pm.
(B) Hold on, please.
(C) On the fourth floor.

（男）　请帮我接分机 470 好吗？
（女）　（A）直到下午 4 点 17 分。
（B）请稍等。
（C）在 4 楼。

12. (Man 1) Would you like to see round the research center?
(Man 2) (A) I’d love to.
(B) Yes, I like it.
(C) No, I won’t.

（男 1） 你想到研究中心各处看看吗？

（男 2） （A）我想去。

（B）是的，我喜欢它。

（C）不，我不会的。

13. (Woman) Do you have any baggage to check, Mr Howard?

(Man) (A) In my checkbook.

(B) Yes, I did.

(C) Just this suitcase.

（女） 哈沃德先生，你有什么行李要托运吗？

（男） （A）在我的支票夹里。

（B）是的，我有过。

（C）就只有这件手提箱。

14. (Man) Do you have any single rooms available?

(Woman) Yes, sir. We still have four vacant rooms this week. How long would you like to stay?

(Man) Just tonight.

（男） 你们还有单人房间可以入住吗？

（女） 是的，先生。本周我们还有 4 个空房间。你想要住多久？

（男） 只是今晚。

15. (Woman) Why don't we go to the movies tomorrow instead of watching TV all day?

(Man) All right. What kind of movie do you want to see?

(Woman) There's a good comedy showing at the Odeon. Performances are at 4:15 and 8:30.

(Man) OK. Let's go to the evening show.

（女）　为什么我们明天不去看电影而要整天看电视呢？

（男）　好啊。你想看什么样的电影？

（女）　欧迪恩剧院有个好看的喜剧上演，演出时间是 4 点 15 分和 8 点半。

（男）　好。我们去看晚上那场吧。

16. (Woman)　And now here's the weather forecast for the next twenty-four hours. It will be mainly dry and sunny but rather cold in the morning with temperatures below zero. You can expect some rain in the afternoon. So, wrap up warm before leaving home today.

（女）　现在是未来 24 小时天气预报。天气将会以干燥、晴朗为主，但是早晨的温度将会低至零下。下午有可能会下雨。所以，今天离开家时穿着请注意保暖。

17. (Man)　It's almost 9:30. If we don't hurry, we'll miss our plane.

(Woman)　You're right. Do you want to take the bus or the train to go to the airport?

(Man)　I think we'd better take a taxi.

（男）　现在已经快到九点半了。如果我们再不快点儿，我们就会赶不上飞机。

（女）　你说得对。你想坐汽车还是火车到飞机场？

（男）　我觉得我们最好是打辆出租车。

18. (Man 1)　Mr Sakamoto, Welcome to CBN industries. Let me introduce you to Mark Harrison, our sales manager; Douglas Norton, our marketing manager, and Jessica Smith, my personal assistant.

(Man 2) Pleased to meet you.

（男 1） 坂本先生，欢迎你来到 CBN 产业集团。请让我向你介绍马克·哈尔森，我们的销售经理，道格拉斯·诺顿，我们的营销经理，以及杰茜卡·史密斯，我的私人助理。

（男 2） 很高兴见到你们。

小测试 1 — 答案

1.　(C)　一个男人正在穿过街道。他在遛狗，把狗用皮带拴着。（A）那只狗是在走，而不是在跑。选项（B）想用发音相似的 working 和 walking 制造混淆。选项（D）并没有准确表述图中动作。

2.　(A)　一个男人正坐在长椅上读报纸。选项（B）想用发音相似的 writing 和 reading 制造混淆。选项（C）那个男人正坐在长椅上，而不是在火车上。（D）长椅上只坐着一个人。

3.　(D)　板条箱堆叠在卡车外面。（A）在卡车附近是有两个人，但是他们并不是在往卡车上装货物。（B）并不能从图中看出两个人正在搬运箱子。（C）没有人正在 climbing into the truck。

4.　(A)　图片表明一群人聚集在一起，听一名歌手和几位演奏师在舞台上表演。（B）没有任何迹象表明音乐会已经结束。选项（C）人们正在等待公交车是把地点和行为弄错了。（D）舞台上不是空的，能看到几个人正在舞台上表演。

5.　(D)　在图片中，有两个孩子站在一个女人面前，女人正看着其中的一个孩子。（A）两个孩子正看着女人。孩子的手中没有书或杂志，所以他们不可能正在阅读什么东西。（B）图片中看不出来女人手里拿着什么东西。（C）图片中没有马。

6.　(C)　问题问的是动作进行的频率。只有选项（C）表明频率。选项（A）回答的是有关“如何”的问题。（B）回答的是有关“在哪里”的问题。

7.　(C)　这道题的关键词是“How long”。疑问词后面的动词是现在完成时，因此直到今天的一段时间，for twenty years，是正确答案。选项（A）表明的是一段距离，而不是直到现在的一段时间。（B）表明的是过去的一段时间。

8. (B) 问题问的是关于地点的信息。选项（A）回答的是关于"when"的问题。选项（C）说明的是开会的目的。

9. (C) 问题是一般现在时，助动词 do 必须用在有 yes 的简短回答中。（A）在有 yes 或 no 简短回答中，不可以缺少宾语而重复动词。（B）am 这个助动词在此不合适。

10. (A) 问题问的是女人是否等了很长时间。间接回答的"只有几分钟"表明她并没有等很长时间。选项（B）回答的是关于距离的问题。（C）回答的是 where 的问题。

11. (B) 问题是一个礼貌的请求。男人想与分机为 470 的人通话。女人请他别挂电话是让他稍等一下。选项（A）和（C）是将分机号 470 混淆成发音相似的时间 4：17 和楼层数 4 楼。

12. (A) 第一个男人问第二个男人是否想参观研究中心。选项（A）有助动词 would，是与提问相符的。（B）选项是一般现在时的普通陈述，与语境不符。（C）有助动词 won't，用在这里是不合适的。

13. (C) 女人想知道哈沃德先生是否有行李要托运。选项（C）他解释说他只有一件手提箱。选项（A）回答的是一个关于地点的问题。选项（B）是一般过去时，不适合回答一般现在时的问题。

14. (B) 那个男人表示他只是今晚入住，也就是只住一晚。对话中没有选项（A）一周和（C）两晚的信息。（D）在这个对话中，4 是指空房间的数量，不是指入住天数。

15. (D) 只有晚上 8：30 有一场演出。女人建议说明天再去看演出，不是（A）今天或者（B）今晚。男人选择了一场晚上的演出，而不是（C）下午的演出。

16. (C) 录音中说听众可以预期下午有雨，这表明天气将会是潮湿的。选项（A）在广播中没有提到。选项（B）晴朗和（D）干燥描述了早上的天气，而不是下午的天气。

17.　(C)　男人决定乘坐出租车，而不是（A）火车或（B）公交车。选项（D）步行在对话中没有提到。

18.　(D)　杰茜卡 · 史密斯为 CBN 企业集团工作。男人介绍她是自己的私人助理。因此她不会是像坂本先生一样的（A）来访者，也不会是马克 · 哈尔森或道格拉斯 · 诺顿一样的（B）经理。（C）坂本先生正在参观史密斯女士工作的公司，这意味着他们不可能是同事。

19.　(A)　Can 是一个用来请求允许做某事的情态动词。助动词（B）have 和（D）had 后面应该跟动词的过去分词。由于问题的主语是第一人称，因此（C）选项的助动词在这里用第三人称单数是不合适的。

20.　(A)　动词 want 后面应该是宾语再加上 to 引导的动词不定式。选项（B）的一般现在时 comes 以及（C）、（D）的动名词形式 coming 用在 want 后面都是错误的。

21.　(A)　介词 before 后面应该用动词的动名词形式。选项（B）to found 是不定式形式。选项（C）是发音相近的动词 find，用在这个语境是不合适的。选项（D）founded 是一般过去时或过去分词。

22.　(D)　在这句话中，动词应该用复数形式，才能与复数的主语 students 保持一致。（A）关系代词 who 应该用来连接两个句子成分，而不应该用主格代词 they。（B）watching 后面不能跟介词 to。（C）动词的数应该与复数主语 students 保持一致。正确的形式应该是 are listening。

23.　(B)　副词 still 应该用在这个句子里，来表明动作还没有结束。（A）介词 until 通常后面跟具体的时间。（C）副词 again 通常用来指重复的场景或动作，而不表示没有完成的场景或动作。（D）ever 一般用在问题中，或是有否定形式动词的句子中。

24. (C) 在这个句子中，应该使用名词性物主代词 theirs 以避免名词 company 的重复使用。（A）They 是主格的人称代词。（B）Their 是形容词性物主代词，后面必须接名词。（D）There's 不能用在这个语境中。

25. (C) 这个句子是关于学校系统的一般陈述。因此，一般现在时的动词形式 go 应该用在这里。选项（A）has gone 和（B）have gone 都是现在完成时。选项（D）is going 是现在进行时，不适合用来陈述一般情况。

26. (A) 只有 on 是可以与 concentrate 正确搭配使用的介词，选项（B）to,（C）at,（D）like 都不能与 concentrate 搭配使用。

27. (A) from 是唯一一个可以用在 borrow money 后面的介词，因此排除选项（B）at,（C）after 和（D）to。

28. (C) born 用在助动词 was 后面用来指过去某一特定时间发生的事情。（A）born 前面必须有助动词 be。（B）事情发生在过去的一个时间，1978 年，就是说助动词 be 应该用过去时，而不是现在时或是（D）的现在完成时。

29. (A) 广告陈述说 Doobie's corner 是一个提供饮料的地方，表明这个地方是一个酒吧。（B）广告里没提到办公室。尽管有大电视屏幕在播出体育节目，但是 Doobie's corner 既不是（C）运动队也不是（D）电视频道。

30. (D) 广告里提到所有的饮料将会半价出售，也就是比平常便宜 50%，因此排除选项（A）更昂贵。（B）Doobie's 酒吧下午 5:00 营业，因此它不可能在这个时间歇业。（C）广告中提到 DJ 是周四的晚上 11:00 开始表演，而不是下午 5:00 到晚上 8:30。

31. (B) 通告说在上午 7:00 至下午 9:00 提供洗熨服务，但是除了周日。因此排除选项（A）每天和（C）周日。（D）洗熨服务只有在上午 7:00 至晚上 9:00 提供，也就表明这不是 24 小时服务。

32.　(C)　每件被取走的衣服要额外支付 5 美元，就是说加急洗熨服务要更贵一些。（A）通告表明衣服必须在中午 12:00 之前拿走，也就是会在下午之前。（B）衣服将在中午 12:00 之前取走，并将在同一天送回，而不是第二天。（D）通告解释说宾馆 cannot be held responsible 为某种 incidents，这就说明洗熨服务不承担所有意外情况的后果。

33.　(B)　这个通告的目的是告知住在宾馆里的客人关于洗熨服务的信息。通告包含了哪天和什么时间提供洗熨服务以及如何提供洗熨服务。（A）宾馆取衣服是洗熨衣服而不是卖掉它们。（C）five dollars 是如果使用加急洗熨服务的话需要多付的钱。（D）信息没有出现在通告中。

34.　(C)　介词 To 出现在表格顶部表明这是一则给 Mike Osborne 的信息。（A）Grace O'Neil 有可能是接电话并写下留言的人。（B）Alison Mc Guire 是那个打电话并留下信息给 Osborne 的女人。（D）Ed Powell 是 Alison Mc Guire 的老板。

35.　(C)　这条信息表明 Powell 先生还没有收到他期待 Mike Osborne 发给他的目录，也就是说目录丢失了。（A）Mc Guire 女士感谢 Osborne 先生发送了 InterCam contract 和（B）the minutes of last week's meeting，这表明她已经收到合同和会议记录，即它们并没有丢失。（D）invoice 这个词没有提到。

小测试 2 — 听力文本

1.

(A) The ladder is in the truck.
(B) The ladder is leaning against the truck.
(C) A man is climbing the ladder.
(D) The truck doors are shut.

（A）梯子在卡车里。

（B）梯子靠在卡车上放着。

（C）一个男人正在爬梯子。

（D）卡车的门是关上的。

2.

(A) All the luggage is on board.
(B) They are boarding the plane.
(C) The runway is bordered by tall trees.
(D) The plane is landing.

（A）所有的行李都已经装上飞机了。

（B）他们正在登机。

（C）跑道的两边上种着高高的树。

（D）飞机正在着陆。

3.

(A) The grass is being cut.
(B) There are some flowers in the park.
(C) There is some flour in the pot.
(D) The children are picking flowers.

（A）草坪正在被修剪。

（B）公园里有一些花。
（C）罐子里有些面粉。
（D）孩子们正在采花。

4.

(A) They are plowing the fields.
(B) They are digging a hole.
(C) They are carrying baskets.
(D) They are not bareheaded.

（A）他们正在犁地。
（B）他们正在挖洞。
（C）他们正在抬篮子。
（D）他们没有光着头。

5. (Woman) Do you know where you parked your car?

(Man) (A) Near the bank.
(B) I can't find them anywhere.
(C) I'll take the bus.

（女） 你知道你把车停在哪里了吗?

（男） （A）在银行旁边。
（B）我到处找不到它们。
（C）我会去坐公交车。

6. (Woman 1) When was Joanna born?

(Woman 2) (A) In 1984.
(B) For 10 years.
(C) In Boston.

（女 1） 乔安娜什么时候出生的?

（女 2） （A）1984 年。
（B）已经 10 年了。

（C）在波士顿。

7. (Woman) Where did you leave your passport?

(Man) (A) I live in Portland.
(B) Two weeks ago.
(C) In a drawer.

（女） 你把护照落在哪里了？

（男） （A）我住在波特兰。
（B）两周之前。
（C）在一个抽屉里。

8. (Man 1) Has she visited the new art gallery?

(Man 2) (A) Yes, he has.
(B) She's been there once.
(C) There's no admission fee.

（男 1） 她参观过那个新的美术馆吗？

（男 2） （A）是的，他参观过。
（B）她去过那里一次。
（C）不需要入场费。

9. (Woman 1) Who is the new instructor?

(Woman 2) (A) He's in the main office.
(B) His name is Paul Andrews.
(C) Yes, we hired a new instructor.

（女 1） 谁是新教练？

（女 2） （A）他在主办公室里。
（B）他的名字是保罗·安德鲁斯。
（C）是的，我们雇了一位新教练。

10. (Woman) Why did the conference begin so late?

(Man) (A) At nine twenty.

(B)　On flowers and birds.
(C)　There was a power failure.

（女）　会议为什么开始得这么晚?

（男）　（A）在 9：20。
（B）在花和鸟上。
（C）供电方面出了问题。

11.　(Man)　When will dinner be ready?

(Woman)　(A)　In about half an hour.
(B)　At an Italian restaurant.
(C)　I haven't read the menu.

（男）　晚餐什么时候准备好?

（女）　（A）半小时之后。
（B）在一个意大利餐厅。
（C）我还没看菜单。

12.　(Woman)　Did Mr Sanchez attend our last meeting?

(Man)　(A)　Last Wednesday.
(B)　No, he couldn't come.
(C)　In Singapore.

（女）　桑切斯先生参加我们上一次的会议了吗?

（男）　（A）上周三。
（B）没有，他来不了。
（C）在新加坡。

13.　(Woman)　Did you walk to the station this morning?

(Man)　(A)　I work at the station.
(B)　I woke up at six this morning.
(C)　No, I took the bus.

（女）　今天早上你是步行去的车站吗?

（男）　（A）我在车站工作。
（B）我今天早上六点醒来的。
（C）没有，我坐了公交车。

14. (Woman 1) Why did he wash your car?

(Woman 2) (A) He watched it last Saturday.
(B) I left my watch in your car.
(C) Because it was dirty.

（女 1）　他为什么要洗你的车？

（女 2）　（A）上周六他看着车。
（B）我把手表落你车上了。
（C）因为车脏了。

15. (Man 1) Good evening. Do you have a reservation?
(Man 2) No, we don't. But we'd like a table for two, please.
(Man 1) Certainly. Please come this way. Your waiter will be with you in a moment.

（男 1）　晚上好，你有预订吗？
（男 2）　没有，我们没预订。但是我们想要一张两人的桌子。
（男 1）　当然。请走这边。侍者马上就过来。

16. (Woman) How long do you want to keep the car?
(Man) Three days. I need it on Friday morning to go to Florida. Do you think I can drop it off there at the end of the weekend and fly back to Philadelphia?
(Woman) Actually, You can leave it at any of our offices in Florida. But there's an extra ten-dollar charge for not returning it where you picked it up.

（女）　这辆车你想用多久？
（男）　三天。我周五上午用这辆车去佛罗里达。你认为我可以在周末把车放在那里，然后再乘飞机回费城吗？
（女）　事实上，你可以将车放在我们在佛罗里达的任何一个办事处。但是你要多付 10 美元费用，因为没有把车归还到你取车的地方。

17. (Man 1) Hi Stuart. Good to see you again, Stuart. How was your trip?
(Man 2) Not too bad. But I'm afraid I'm late. My plane took off late due to bad weather conditions in Toronto.
(Man 1) That's OK. The meeting hasn't started yet. We still have to wait for the Chairman whose car got stuck in a traffic jam.

（男 1） 你好，斯图亚特。很高兴再次见到你，斯图亚特。你的旅行怎么样？
（男 2） 还不错。但是恐怕我迟到了。在多伦多我的航班因为天气原因起飞晚了。
（男 1） 没关系。会议还没开始呢。我们还得等会议的主席，他的车遇到交通堵塞了。

18. (Woman) Good morning Frank. This is Kim Adams. I've just received a copy of your report. Can we meet on Wednesday to review it?
(Man) Well, I'm flying to Boston this afternoon. And I'm afraid I won't be back until Thursday. So, why don't we meet the next day?
(Woman) Fine. I'll see you then.

（女） 早上好，弗兰克。我是金姆·亚当斯。我刚收到你的一份报告。我们周三的时候能见面讨论一下吗？
（男） 噢，我今天下午飞波士顿。恐怕周四之前回不来。那么，我们周五见面好吗？
（女） 好的，我们到时候见。

19. (Man) I'm looking for a sweater for a nine-year old girl.
(Woman) What size is she?
(Man) Ten, if I remember well.
(Woman) You will find a selection of sweaters on the sixth floor.

（男） 我想给一个 9 岁的女孩买一件毛衣。
（女） 她穿什么尺码？
（男） 10 码，如果我没记错的话。

（女） 你会在6层找到各种毛衣。

20. (Man) Why do I have to put out my cigarette?
(Woman) This is a non-smoking flight, sir. Actually, all our flights are non-smoking.
(Man) Oh! I'm sorry. I didn't know.

（男） 为什么我非得熄灭香烟？
（女） 先生，这是禁烟航班。事实上，我们所有的航班都是禁烟的。
（男） 噢，抱歉！我原来不知道。

小测试 2 — 答案

1.　(B)　图片上是一辆卡车停在了一个建筑物前。一架梯子顶着卡车门放着。（A）梯子是放在卡车外面，而不是里面。（C）没有人正在爬，也就是上到梯子上。（D）卡车的门只关了一个，另一个门是开着的。

2.　(B)　图片中有一些乘客正在登机，也就是他们正在走上飞机。（A）图片并没有表明飞机上装了什么货物，也就是有什么东西在飞机里面。然而，我们能看到背景上有一些行李放在地上，也就是说并不是所有的行李都已经装载完成了。（C）图片中看不到树。（D）既然乘客们还在登机，那么飞机也就不可能正在着陆，也就是不可能在空中飞行后落到地面上。

3.　(B)　在图片中，背景上我们能看到一些树，前面有一些花。（A）尽管草坪很短，但是没有人正在进行修剪工作。选项（C）是用发音相近的 flour 和 flower 造成混淆。（D）图片中看不到孩子。

4.　(D)　图片中的两个人物头上都戴着东西，因此他们没有光着头。尽管两人站在田地里，但是他们并没有在（A）耕地，也没有在（B）挖洞。（C）图片中看不到有篮子。

5.　(A)　问题是问停车的位置。选项（A）表明男子将车停在了银行旁边。选项（B）用了复数人称代词 them，这与单数名词 car 不相符。选项（C）回答的是出行方式问题，而不是汽车的位置。

6.　(A)　关键词是 when，所以日期是正确答案。选项（B）10 年是一段时间，不是日期，（C）波士顿是一个地点，不是日期。

7.　(C)　问题是护照落在哪里了，选项（C）表明男人把它落在了抽屉里，选项（B）回答的事过去一段时间的问题，选项（A）把发音近似的动词 live 和 leave 弄混了。

8.　(B)　第一个男人想知道是否有一个女人来参观了新画廊，第二个男人回答说她已经来过一次了。选项（A）主格代词 he 表示是一个男性，而不是题中提到的女性。选项（C）提到入场费，与语境无关。

9.　(B)　问题中的关键词是 who，所以问题应该涉及人。只有选项 B 提供了适合的答案。选项（A）回答了教练在哪里，而不是他是谁，选项（C）回答了一个闭合问题。

10.　(C)　问题问的是原因，会议为什么没有按时举行。选项（C）解释了是供电的原因，选项（A）回答的是什么时候或什么时间，而不是为什么，选项（B）回答的问题是关于什么，而不是为什么。

11.　(A)　问题问的是时间，只有选项（A）提供了正确的答案。选项（B）是地点，而不是时间，选项（C）弄混了近音词 read 和 ready。

12.　(B)　问题问的是桑切斯先生是否出席了会议，选项（B）暗示他没有出席，选项（A）回答了是什么时候，选项（C）回答了关于地点的问题。

13.　(C)　问题问的是男人是否步行去的车站，他解释说他是坐公交车去的车站，而不是步行，选项（A）和（B）弄混了发音近似的 work, woke 和 walk。

14.　(C)　问题问为什么洗车了，选项（C）解释车很脏，这意味着车需要清洗，选项（A）和（B）弄混了近音词 watch 和 wash。

15.　(C)　说话者使用了 table 和 waiter，这暗示发生的场景是饭店而不是（A）在机场,（B）在飞机上或（D）在家具商店。

16.　(A)　男人提及了他需要用三天车，女人告诉他归还时需要付额外费用，这些细节暗示这个男人要租车。选项（B）弄混了近音词组 rent a car 和 send a card，选项（C）中的 10 美元是因为不能把车返回费城而额外付的，选项（D）男人想乘车去佛罗里达，而不是坐飞机。

17. (B) 斯图亚特解释他的飞机由于多伦多的坏天气而起飞晚了，（A）他的航班推迟了，但他没有错过，（C）是主席而不是斯图亚特遇到交通堵塞了，（D）斯图亚特迟到是因为坏天气，而不是因为主席。

18. (D) 女人建议第二天即周五和弗兰克见面，（A）男人要在今天下午飞去波士顿，暗示他不能在那个时间见女人。男人周三（B）和周四（C）都将在波士顿。

19. (C) 男人提及女孩 9 岁。选项（A）six 指的是男人能找到毛衣的楼层，选项（B）eight 这个单词在对话中没有被提到。选项（D）ten 是女孩的尺码，而不是年龄。

20. (A) 女人提及 fight 航班这个单词，表明说话者在飞机上，选项（B）在公交车上，选项（C）在火车上，选项（D）在酒吧，这些并未在对话中提及。

小测试 3 — 答案

1. (A) with 是可以与短语 Do you agree 连用的唯一正确的介词。排除（B）at,（C）to 和（D）for。

2. (A) 连词 unless 意味着“except if”应当用于这个句子中。（B）however 和（C）although 用在这里不合适，因为它们通常用于比较两种观点,（D）中的连词 since 通常暗示某种情况或动作发生在过去，并仍在进行。

3. (B) because of 应用于此句中，介绍航班取消的原因。（A）despite 和（D）whereas 一般用于比较两种观点,（C）instead of 一般用来指另一种选择。

4. (A) 副词 ever 应当用于这个问题中,（B）中的副词 never 不能用于问题中,（C）either 一般用于指某种选择,（D）副词 again 一般用于某种反复的情景或动作中。

5. (D) invoice 是补充这句话的正确词汇，因为它是一个可数名词，并且它可接在冠词 an 的后面。（A）advice 和（B）information 都是不可数名词，也就是说它们不可数，不能接在冠词 an 的后面。（C）可数名词 form 不可以接在不定冠词 an 的后面，因为 an 通常用于元音前。

6. (C) 形容词 interested 构成短语 not very interested in politics，它用来形容人们的感受，而选项（D）interesting 是现在分词，用来形容造成此种感受的人，选项（A）bored 和（B）boring 不能放在介词 in 的前面。

7. (A) lose 意思是不再拥有某物是因为你不知道它在哪里，所以在这里是正确选项。选项（C）loses 是第三人称单数，不能放在主格代词 you 之后，选项（B）形容词 loose 和选项（D）名词

loss 发音相近，在这里都不可能出现。

8. (C) 名词 personnel 构成短语 personnel manager 表达一部门种类，选项（A）名词 person 指一个人，选项（D）名词 personality 表示一个人的情感和行为特征，无法表达 personnel 要表达的含义，尽管选项（B）形容词 personal 与 personnel 发音相似，但它指的是与私人相关的事物，并不是指某公司的职员。

9. (A) 此问句为一般现在时，频率副词 usually 位于动词之前，选项（B）中 does 是提问宾语时一般现在时的标志，动词形式要省略 to 的不定式，选项（C）和（D）中的助动词没有放在主语 Luke 之前。

10. (C) 形容词 economical 说明这辆车是经济实用型，也就是说这辆车不用花太多钱加油和保养，按照语法规则，用连词比如 but 连接的词或词组，必须保持相同的语法形式（这里指的是词性相同）。因此，排除选项（A）中的名词 economy 和选项（D）中的副词 economically。选项（B）中的形容词 economic 指的是经济、财富和物质上的需求，而 economical 指的是节约的，不浪费的。

11. (D) 这是一则招聘启事。选项（A）中，虽然这则招聘启事不是招聘人力资源部的管理人员，而是杂志社的编辑助理，但求职者需将自己的求职申请送至人力资源部，选项（B）中虽然拥有与出版相关的软件知识很有必要，但是广告招聘的不是软件设计人员，选项（C）中虽然熟练掌握英语及其他两门外语很有必要，但广告并未说招聘的是语言教师。

12. (C) 广告中提到要熟练掌握除英语以外的至少两门外语，说明求职者需要懂好几门外语。选项（A）广告中并未对求职者的外貌做出要求，选项（B）less 和 at least 虽然听起来一样，实则意思大相径庭：at least three years 意思是三年及以上，而 less than three years 指一或两年。选项（D）文中未提到驾驶执照。

13. (B) 文中提到这个公司在其领域居于领先的地位。（A）中重视截止时间是要求求职者，而不是公司。（C）虽然广告中多次提到 history 一词，但并未提到该公司出版与历史相关的杂志。（D）中公司要求求职者懂得与出版相关的软件知识，并不是公司涉及软件开发。

14. (A) 广告中提到求职者需将求职申请发送至何处，也暗示求职者与公司联系需通过邮寄，而选项（B）中电子邮件的地址、选项（C）中传真号、选项（D）中电话号码在文中均未提及。

15. (B) 这个表格用于收集信息，帮助组织考试的部门提高考试的质量。选项（A）是取消考试，选项（C）是宣布考试时间，选项（D）是一份调查问卷，用于问问题，而不是回答问题。

16. (A) 其中的一个问题指的是考试准备课程，因此表格是为参加考试的人设定的，而不是选项（B）监考人员，选项（C）老师。选项（D）中虽然问题里重复出现 industry 一词，但并未提及 industrialists，即管理工厂或经营公司的商人。

17. (B) 在他的回答中，夏帕德先生提到了他的公司，也就是说他不是一名学生。选项（A）并未提到他参加考试的次数，选项（C）在表格中并未提到这点，选项（D）夏帕德先生在第 5 个问题中提到他的公司交了注册费。

18. (B) 文中提到在 10 月 14 日要做完所有的事，完成所有的任务。选项（A）预订火车票，选项（C）电话号码，选项（D）书名，这些文中皆未提及。文中的book作动词，意思是预订，而不是作名词。

19. (C) 清单中提到今天要预订帝国酒店的房间。选项（A）是下周开会，不是今天。选项（B）错误，因为清单中表明今天的演讲被迫取消。选项（D）错误，因为计划与田中先生吃商务午餐，而不是商务晚餐。

20. (B) 穆勒先生要在今天上午10:30打电话。选项（A）勒克莱尔先生要去接电话，不是打电话。文中没有提到选项（C）苏珊娜或选项（D）田中先生要打电话。

模拟测试 1 — 听力文本

1.

(A) A child has given some money to the musician.
(B) A crowd has gathered around the musician.
(C) The orchestra is playing some music.
(D) The musician is holding an instrument.

（A）一个孩子已经给了演奏者一些钱。
（B）一群人已经围住演奏者。
（C）管弦乐队正在演奏音乐。
（D）演奏者正拿着一件乐器。

2.

(A) They are waiting for the bus.
(B) They are walking through a wood.
(C) They have lost their way.
(D) They are crossing the street.

（A）他们在等公交车。
（B）他们正穿过一片树林。
（C）他们已经迷路了。
（D）他们正横穿街道。

3.

(A) The animals are in a cage.
(B) The cage is open.
(C) The birds are in their nest.
(D) The animals are drinking.

（A）动物们在笼子里。
（B）笼子是打开的。

（C）鸟儿们在它们的窝里。

（D）动物们正在喝水。

4.

(A)　The man is playing the piano.
(B)　He is typing letters.
(C)　He is facing a screen.
(D)　The computers are out of order.

（A）那个男人正在弹钢琴。

（B）他正在打信件。

（C）他正面对着屏幕。

（D）电脑都坏了。

5.

(A)　The people are getting off the bus.
(B)　The people are boarding the bus.
(C)　The bus driver is speaking to a passenger.
(D)　The doors are not open.

（A）人们正在下公交车。

（B）人们正在上公交车。

（C）公交车司机正在与一名乘客交谈。

（D）门都没开。

6.

(A)　They are hunting.
(B)　They are sailing.
(C)　They are frying fish.
(D)　They are fishing.

（A）他们正在打猎。

（B）他们正在航行。

（C）他们正在煎鱼。

（D）他们正在钓鱼。

7.

(A) The birds are making a nest.
(B) The birds are all on the steps.
(C) A woman is feeding the birds.
(D) The birds are in a cage.

（A）鸟儿们正在筑巢。

（B）鸟儿们都落在台阶上。

（C）一个女人正在喂鸟。

（D）鸟儿们都在笼子里。

8.

(A) There is a spoon in the cup.
(B) The saucer is under the cup.
(C) The saucer is above the cup.
(D) The cup is empty.

（A）杯子里有一个勺子。

（B）杯碟在杯子下面。

（C）杯碟在杯子上面。

（D）这个杯子是空的。

9.

(A) The girls are sitting next to one another.
(B) They are facing a building.
(C) They are studying.
(D) They are looking at a map.

（A）女孩们彼此紧挨着坐着。

（B）她们正面对着一个建筑。

（C）她们正在学习。

（D）她们正在看地图。

10.

(A) The cars are waiting at the traffic lights.
(B) The cars are parked.

(C)　The cards are packed.
(D)　The traffic is congested.

（A）汽车正在等交通信号灯。
（B）汽车是停着的。
（C）卡片是包装好的。
（D）交通拥堵。

11.
(A)　The bottles are in boxes.
(B)　The bottles are lined up.
(C)　Only one bottle is labeled.
(D)　The bottles are broken.

（A）瓶子都在盒子里。
（B）瓶子排成一行。
（C）只有一个瓶子被贴上了标签。
（D）瓶子被打碎了。

12.
(A)　The table is empty.
(B)　There are several bottles on the table.
(C)　There aren't any glasses on the table.
(D)　The table has been set.

（A）桌子是空的。
（B）在桌子上有一些瓶子。
（C）在桌子上没有玻璃杯。
（D）桌面上的东西已经摆好。

13.
(A)　The woman is riding a bicycle.
(B)　The woman is reading a book about bicycles.
(C)　The woman is getting rid of her bicycle.
(D)　The bicycle is in front of a bus.

（A）那个女人正在骑一辆自行车。
（B）那个女人正在读一本关于自行车的书。
（C）那个女人正摆脱她的自行车。
（D）那辆自行车在一辆公交车前面。

14.
(A)　The woman looked at the items.
(B)　The woman is looking at the items.
(C)　She is entering the store.
(D)　She is leaving the store.

（A）那个女人看了货品。
（B）那个女人正在看货品。
（C）她正走进商店。
（D）她正离开商店。

15.
(A)　The man is filming a scene.
(B)　The man is watching a movie.
(C)　They're filling out forms.
(D)　They're exchanging films.

（A）那个男人正在拍摄一个场景。
（B）那个男人正在看一场电影。
（C）他们正在填写表格。
（D）他们正在换胶卷。

16.　(Woman)　Can you confirm your booking by fax?

(Man)　(A)　I need the books.
(B)　I can't read it.
(C)　Sure. What's your fax number?

（女）　你能通过传真确认你的预订吗？

（男）　（A）我需要书籍。
（B）我不能读它。

（C）当然，你的传真号码是什么？

17. (Man) Would you like a starter?

(Woman) (A) I'll have Chef salad, please.
(B) Yes, I love it.
(C) I would like to start now.

（男） 你想要开胃菜吗？

（女） （A）我想要主厨特制沙拉，谢谢。
（B）是的，我喜欢。
（C）我想现在就开始。

18. (Woman) Do you like spicy food?

(Man) (A) Yes, I would.
(B) Not very much.
(C) It looks like fish.

（女） 你喜欢辛辣的食物吗？

（男） （A）是的，我愿意。
（B）不是非常喜欢。
（C）它看起来像鱼。

19. (Man) Would you like a wake-up call tomorrow morning?

(Woman) (A) Yes, I do.
(B) Yes, at 7:00 please.
(C) I woke up at 7:00.

（男） 明天早上你想要叫早服务吗？

（女） （A）是的，我是。
（B）是的，请在 7 点。
（C）我 7 点醒了。

20. (Man) Good morning, Christina. How are you?

(Woman) (A) Yes, I am.
(B) Steve's sister.
(C) Fine, thanks.

（男） 早上好，克里斯蒂娜，你好吗？

（女） （A）是的，我是。
（B）史蒂夫的姐姐。
（C）很好，谢谢。

21. (Man) Did you go to the conference last week?

(Woman) (A) In Barcelona.
(B) It lasted two days.
(C) I couldn't make it.

（男） 上个星期你去参加会议了吗？

（女） （A）在巴塞罗那。
（B）它持续了两天。
（C）我没有赶到。

22. (Woman 1) Will you excuse me a moment?

(Woman 2) (A) After the meeting.
(B) Yes, sure.
(C) Pleased to meet you.

（女 1） 我失陪一会儿好吗？

（女）2 （A）在会议之后。
（B）当然可以。
（C）很高兴见到你。

23. (Woman) How are you finding your room?

(Man) (A) It's too small.
(B) I found it in the bathroom.
(C) Very pleased.

（女）　你感觉房间如何？

（男）　（A）它太小了。
（B）我在浴室找到它的。
（C）很高兴。

24. (Man)　Who is the new sales manager?

(Woman)　(A)　In Canada.
(B)　Since last year.
(C)　Walter's wife.

（男）　谁是新的销售经理？

（女）　（A）在加拿大。
（B）自从去年。
（C）沃尔特的妻子。

25. (Man 1)　What time did the plane land?

(Man 2)　(A)　At seven.
(B)　Seven times.
(C)　The seventh time.

（男 1）　飞机什么时间降落的？

（男 2）　（A）在七点。
（B）七次。
（C）第七次。

26. (Woman)　How many of you are coming?

(Man)　(A)　Twice.
(B)　Both of us.
(C)　By train.

（女）　你们要来几个人？

（男）　（A）两次。
（B）我们两个人。

（C）坐火车。

27. (Man) Who are you buying this tie for?

(Woman)
(A) At a gift shop.
(B) I'm tied up all day.
(C) My brother-in-law.

（男）你买这条领带给谁？

（女）
（A）在一个礼品商店。
（B）我被整天绑起来。
（C）我的小叔子。

28. (Man) How would you like to pay for this?

(Woman)
(A) 20 dollars.
(B) Yes, I would.
(C) By check.

（男）你想怎样支付这个？

（女）
（A）20美元。
（B）是的，我会的。
（C）用支票。

29. (Woman) Is there a fax machine on the second floor?

(Man)
(A) No. She's on the third floor.
(B) Five minutes ago.
(C) I don't think so.

（女）二楼有传真机吗？

（男）
（A）不，她在三楼。
（B）五分钟以前。
（C）我想应该没有。

30. (Man) What would you like to drink with your meal?

(Woman)　(A)　I don't like meat.
(B)　We can meet there if you like.
(C)　I'll have some soda.

（男）　用餐的时候你喜欢喝点什么饮料？

（女）　（A）我不喜欢肉。
（B）如果你喜欢，我们可以在那里见面。
（C）我想要一些苏打水。

31.　(Man)　Who sent her an e-mail?

(Woman)　(A)　The accountant did.
(B)　She sent it to the post office.
(C)　There's one in the center.

（男）　谁给她发电子邮件了？

（女）　（A）会计师发的。
（B）她发送它到邮局。
（C）中心有一个。

32.　(Man)　Can we meet at 9:00 tomorrow morning?

(Woman)　(A)　We met at 9:20.
(B)　9 o'clock is fine.
(C)　I can't eat that.

（男）　我们可以在明天早上 9 点见面吗？

（女）　（A）我们在 9:20 见过。
（B）9 点可以。
（C）我不能吃那个。

33.　(Woman)　Do you have any plans for this weekend?

(Man)　(A)　I played golf last weekend.
(B)　The plane leaves at 4:50.
(C)　I'd like to go fishing.

（女）　这周末你有安排吗？

（男）　（A）我上周末打了高尔夫球。
（B）飞机在 4:50 起飞。
（C）我想去钓鱼。

34. (Woman)　Which platform does your train leave from?

(Man)　(A) It leaves at 5:00.
(B) I live near the train station.
(C) The one on the left.

（女）　你的火车从哪个站台出发？

（男）　（A）5 点出发。
（B）我住在火车站附近。
（C）左边的那个。

35. (Woman)　When did you come back from Lisbon?

(Man)　(A) Next week.
(B) Last Saturday.
(C) To Tokyo.

（女）　你什么时候从里斯本回来的？

（男）　（A）下周。
（B）上周六。
（C）到东京。

36. (Man 1)　Good morning, sir. Have you got anything to declare?
(Man 2)　No. I'm only here on business for a few days.
(Man 1)　Then I guess you won't mind opening your case.

（男 1）　早上好，先生。你有什么要申报的吗？
（男 2）　没有。我只是到这里出差几天。
（男 1）　那么我想你应该不介意打开你的行李箱。

37. (Woman)　Jeff, can you take me to the shopping mall?
(Man)　I'm sorry but I can't. My car broke down yesterday.

(Woman)　That's OK. I'll take the bus.

(女)　杰夫，你能带我去购物中心吗？
(男)　很抱歉，但是我不能带你去。我的汽车昨天坏了。
(女)　没问题，我坐公交车去。

38. (Man)　When will dinner be served?
(Woman)　A few minutes after take off. But I can get you something to drink now if you like.
(Man)　That's very kind of you. I'd like a glass of water, please.

(男)　晚餐什么时候开始提供？
(女)　起飞之后几分钟就开始了。但是如果你想要的话，我现在就可以给你拿点儿喝的来。
(男)　你太好了。我想要一杯水，谢谢。

39. (Woman)　The accountant is waiting for you in your office.
(Man)　Thanks Maria. Are there any new messages for me?
(Woman)　Yes. Ms Simons called three times this morning. She said that the next committee meeting is set for Thursday at 5:00pm.

(女)　会计在你的办公室等你。
(男)　谢谢玛利亚。还有给我的新信息吗？
(女)　是的，西蒙斯女士今天早晨打了三次电话。她说下一次委员会会议定在周四下午 5 点。

40. (Woman)　What's the quickest way downtown?
(Man)　Well, you can take the A38 bus. But if you really want to save time, take a taxi.
(Woman)　OK. I'll do that. Thanks.

(女)　最快到达市中心的交通方式是什么？
(男)　嗯，你可以乘坐 A38 路公交车。但是如果你真的想节省时间，坐出租车吧。
(女)　好的，我会那样做的，谢谢。

41. (Woman) Could I have it back when you've finished reading it?
(Man) Yes, sure. Sorry I forgot I still had it.
(Woman) It's all right. There's no rush. It's just that I met Jerry on the train yesterday and I promised to lend it to him.

（女） 你读完了能还给我吗？
（男） 是的，当然。很抱歉我忘了它仍然在我手里。
（女） 没关系，不着急。只是因为我昨天在火车上看见杰瑞，并答应要借给他。

42. (Woman) This is Barnett Financial Services. Our office is closed at the moment. We are open weekdays between 9:00am and 5:30pm Please leave your name and number after the tone and we'll call you back as soon as the office is open. Thank you.

（女） 这是巴尼特金融服务公司。现在我们的办公室不办公。我们在工作日的办公时间是上午 9 点到下午 5:30。在听到提示音之后，请留下您的名字和电话号码，我们将在办公时间尽快给您回话。谢谢您。

43. (Woman) Where are you from Mr Nishimura?
(Man) I was born in Osaka but I've been living in Tokyo for twenty years.
(Woman) How long are you going to stay in New York?
(Man) Not long. I must leave on Sunday.

（女） 西村先生，你从哪里来？
（男） 我出生在大阪，但我在东京生活了 20 年。
（女） 你准备在纽约待多久？
（男） 不会太久，我周日就得离开。

44. (Woman 1) Do you want me to call a taxi to take you to your hotel after the presentation?
(Woman 2) Is the hotel far?
(Woman 1) Not really. About ten minutes' walk from here.
(Woman 2) So, it's very close. I can easily walk.

（女 1） 讲座之后你想让我叫辆出租车送你到宾馆吗？
（女 2） 宾馆远吗？
（女 1） 不太远，从这里走路大约需要十分钟。
（女 2） 如此说来非常近，我可以轻松走到。

45. (Man) Good morning. Can I speak to Mr Edwards, please?
(Woman) I'm sorry but Mr Edwards no longer works in this department. He was transferred to Research and Development two months ago.
(Man) I see. Can you give me his new number?

（男） 早上好，请问我可以和爱德华先生通话吗？
（女） 很抱歉，爱德华先生已经不在这个部门工作了。他两个月前被调到研发部去了。
（男） 我知道了，你能给我他的新电话号码吗？

46. (Man) Have you bought a present for Cathy's wedding yet?
(Woman) Not yet. But there's still plenty of time.
(Man) Not so much, actually. The ceremony is scheduled for next Saturday.

（男） 你已经给凯西的婚礼准备礼物了吗？
（女） 还没有，但仍然有充足的时间准备。
（男） 事实上也不是很多，仪式被安排在下周六。

47. (Woman) Good morning. I'd like to book a round trip to go to Amsterdam on June 10.
(Man) Yes, Madam. There are two flights from Kennedy airport on that day. At 9:00 am and 11:00pm.
(Woman) OK. I'll take the first one.

（女） 早上好，我想预订 6 月 10 日去阿姆斯特丹的往返机票。
（男） 好的，女士。那天有两班从肯尼迪机场起飞的航班，在早上 9 点和晚上 11 点。
（女） 好的，我要乘坐第一个航班。

48. (Man) Excuse me, Melissa. Do you know where room 225 is?
(Woman) Room 225? I know where it is. Please, come this way.
(Man) That's very kind of you.

（男）打扰了，玛丽莎，你知道 225 房间在哪儿吗？
（女）225 房间？我知道在哪儿，请走这边。
（男）非常感谢。

49. (Woman) Where do I get off for the National Museum?
(Man) It's the last stop.
(Woman) How long does it take to get there?
(Man) Not too long. About ten minutes.

（女）我要去国家博物馆该从哪里下车？
（男）最后一站。
（女）到那里需要多久呢？
（男）没有多久，大约 10 分钟。

50. (Woman) Do you know how to get to the train station?
(Man) If you take a taxi, you'll be there in about twenty minutes.
(Woman) How much will it cost from here?
(Man) No more than nine or ten dollars, I guess.

（女）你知道怎么去火车站吗？
（男）如果你乘坐出租车，到那大约 20 分钟。
（女）从这到那需要花多少钱？
（男）我猜不会超过 9 或 10 美元。

模拟测试 1 — 答案

1.　(D)　照片中一个男人正在用他手中的萨克斯管演奏音乐。（A）在照片中没有小孩。（B）人群是指聚集在一起的一个群体。在图片中，没有人站在音乐演奏者的旁边。（C）这个男人是独自演奏的。他不是由一群音乐演奏者组成的管弦乐队中的一员。

2.　(D)　图片中，人们正在横穿马路，即他们正在从街道的一端走向另一端，因此（A）他们不是在等公交车。（B）这张照片的背景是一个城镇的街道，而不是一片树林。（C）没有证据表明人们迷路了。

3.　(A)　图片中展现了一群鸟待在笼子里。（B）笼子的门是看不见的。（C）鸟儿们不在窝里。鸟窝是指鸟儿或者昆虫修建的一个用来居住、生育或者产卵的地方。（D）从图片中可以看出，尽管两个罐都装满了液体物质，但没有证据表明鸟儿们正在饮用它。

4.　(C)　男人正坐在电脑屏幕前面，或正面对着电脑屏幕。因此排除选项（A）弹钢琴。（B）尽管这个男人正坐在电脑前，但仍然不能表明他正在打信件。（D）图片中只能看见一台电脑。

5.　(B)　图片中展示了一些人正在进入或者正在上一辆公交车。（A）人们正在上，而不是正在下公交车。（C）图片中看不见驾驶公交车的人。（D）门是开着的，以便于乘客上公交车。

6.　(D)　图片中展现了一些人站在一个湖前拿着鱼竿。他们很有可能正在钓鱼，因此不会是（A）在打猎或者（B）在航行。（C）尽管人们正在钓鱼，即努力地去抓鱼，但没有证据表明他们同时正在煎鱼。

7. (B) 图片中所有的鸟儿都站在阶梯的台阶上。（A）它们似乎不是在筑巢，巢通常是指由树枝或草做成的栖息处。（C）图片中没有女人。（D）鸟儿是自由的，没有被锁在笼子里。

8. (B) 图片中显示出有一个杯子，还有一个杯碟在它的下面。（A）在照片中没有勺子。（C）杯碟不是在杯子上面，而是在它下面。（D）没有证据表明杯子是空的或是满的。

9. (A) 三个女孩正紧挨着坐在一起。（B）看不出来她们正面对着建筑物。图片中唯一可见的建筑在她们的身后。（C）看不出来她们正在学习，或者（D）正在看地图。

10. (B) 汽车似乎是停在一个地下停车场。（A）汽车没有在行驶，因此不可能在等交通信号灯。（C）图片中看不到卡片。（D）图片中看不出来交通的状况。

11. (B) 图片中显示一些瓶子排成一行，即 lined up。（A）图片中没有盒子。（C）好几个瓶子上而不只是一个瓶子上有标签。（D）瓶子看上去是完好的，并没有打碎。

12. (D) 桌面上的东西已经摆好，图片显示了类似盘子和玻璃杯等物品已经被排列好，用于用餐。（A）桌子上有几样东西，表明桌子上不是什么都没有。（B）图片中只能看见一个瓶子。（C）图片中可以看到有几个玻璃杯 glasses。

13. (A) 那个女人正在骑自行车，即她坐在自行车上面并且在向一个方向移动。（B）在骑车的同时，她看起来不像在阅读。（C）看不出来她想摆脱自行车。（D）在自行车后面看不见公交车。

14. (B) 那个女人正在看货品，即正在仔细查看展示出来的商品。（A）looked at 是过去式，在这里是不恰当的。（C）她在商店外面，不是正在走进商店或者（D）走出商店。

15. (A) 那个男人正拿着一个照相机，并且用相机拍摄其他人。（B）他没有在屏幕前面，因此他不可能是在看电影。图片里看不到有（C）表格 forms 或（D）胶卷 films。

16. (C) 问题是要求通过传真来确认事情。尽管对于提问没有给出一个直接回答，选项（C）是唯一一个与所给场景相关的回答。选项（A）混淆了发音相似的单词预订 booking 和用来阅读的书籍 books。选项（B）故意不顾语境重复使用了问题中的 can 这个单词。

17. (A) 这个问题询问女人想吃什么。选项（A）表明她想吃主厨特制沙拉 chef salad。（B）问题没有询问女人是否喜欢什么东西。（C）混淆了发音相同的单词开胃菜 starter（名词）和开始 start（动词）。

18. (B) 讲话者询问男人是否喜欢辛辣的食物（spicy food）。选项（B）表明他并不是真的喜欢。（A）助动词 would 不适合回答用 do 开头的一般疑问句。选项（C）回答的是关于食物外观的问题。

19. (B) 男人询问女人是否需要叫早服务，正确的回应表明她是需要的，因为她的回答给出了她希望被叫醒的时间。（A）助动词 do 不适合来回答由 would 引导的一般疑问句。选项（C）用的是一般过去时，而问题中说的是“明天早上”。

20. (C) 只有选项（C）提供了一个适合于问题“你好吗?”的答案。（A）yes 不适合于回答关于“how”这样的问题。选项（B）回答一个关于某一个人身份的问题（在这种情况下，问题应该用“who”而不是用“how”开头）。

21. (C) 男人想知道女人是否参加了会议。I couldn’t make it 意思是女人没能参加会议。选项（A）回答了“where”的问题。选项（B）回答了关于“how long”的问题。

22. (B) 只有选项（B）提供了一个适合问题的答案。选项（A）回答了关于“when”的问题。选项（C）“很高兴认识你”仅用于两个人第一次见面的时候。

23. (A) 疑问词“how”被用来询问男人，他觉得他的房间怎么样。他解释说房间太小了。选项（B）提到了物体的位置，而不是男人关于房间的意见。（C）“很高兴”very pleased 在这个语境中不适合，因为他表达了一种感觉而不是一个意见。

24. (C) 这里关键的疑问词是“who”，所以问题的答案应该涉及一个人。只有选项（C）提供了一个合适的答案。选项（A）回答了一个“where”的问题。选项（B）回答了一个直到现在的时间长度的问题，而不是一个人。

25. (A) 问题询问时间。选项（A）表明飞机是在七点降落的。选项（B）“七次”和（C）“第七次”重复了从问题中而来的单词“时间（time）”，但表示的却是发生的次数。

26. (B) 问题询问了人的数量。both of us 表明了包括说话者在内的两个人。（A）“两次”是指次数，不是人的数量。选项（C）回答了问题“how”而不是“how many”。

27. (C) 这里关键的疑问词是“who”，所以答案应该涉及一个人。只有选项（C）提供了一个合适的答案。选项（A）表明了买领带的地方。选项（B）混淆了发音相似的单词“tie”和“tied”。

28. (C) 问题问的是支付的方法。只有选项（C）用支票提供了一个合适的答案。选项（A）20 美元指出支付的总和。（B）“yes”不适合回答带有“how”的问题。

29. (C) 讲话者解释说他认为二楼没有传真机。（A）主格代词“她”只能指代一个人，而不是机器。选项（B）回答的是关于“how long ago”或者“when”的问题。

30. (C) 这里的疑问词是 what，所以正确的答案是一件东西。选项（A）和（B）混淆了相似发音的单词“meat”（食物）和“meet”（动词），并且这两个词都与饮料无关，所以不是合适的答案。

31. (A) 这里关键的疑问词是“who”，所以答案应该是指一个人。只有选项（A）提供了一个合适的答案。选项（B）回答了“where”的问题。选项（C）混淆了发音相似的短语“sent her”和“center”。

32.　(B)　说话者想知道女人在第二天 9 点是否有时间。她表明 9 点可以，即 9 点对她来说是方便的。选项（A）是过去式，不适合于回答关于将来计划的问题。选项（C）混淆了发音相似的短语“can't eat”和“can...meet”。

33.　(C)　问题询问周末的计划。在他的回答中，男人解释他已经有这周末钓鱼的计划。选项（A）指的是过去，不是未来。选项（B）混淆了发音相似的单词“plans”和“planes”。

34.　(C)　这是一个关于站台信息的问题。选项（C）表明火车预计从左边的站台驶出。选项（A）回答了一个“when” 的问题。选项（B）混淆了发音相似的单词“live”和“leave”。

35.　(B)　问题是一般过去时并且关键词是“when”，所以日期是正确的答案。选项（A）指的是在未来的一段时间，不是在过去。选项（C）回答了一个关于目的地的问题。

36.　(B)　“won't mind + doing”是一个用来要求某人做某事的表达。执法人员想检查男人的行李箱里有什么，所以可以认为男人很有可能会打开它。（A）男人回答说他没有什么东西要申报。说话者没有提到（C）出示护照或者（D）去度假。

37.　(A)　杰夫的问题是他的汽车坏了，意味着汽车不能再开了，不得不送去修理。（B）杰夫不需要去购物中心；女人需要去购物中心。（C）对话没有提及腿受伤。（D）杰夫说他不能带女人去购物中心，而不是他不能开车了。

38.　(A)　女人提到单词 take off“起飞”，take off 是指飞机上升到空中的那一刻。这表明，尽管说话者提到了晚餐时间和饮品，但是对话发生在飞机上而不是（B）在餐厅或（C）在酒吧。（D）对话中没有提到百货商店。

39.　(D)　玛利亚解释说下一次委员会会议被安排在 5 点，或确定在 5 点，而不是（C）3 点。（A）今天早上是西蒙女士接到电话的时间。（B）会议被安排在 Thursday 周四，而不是相似发音的

Tuesday 周二。

40. (C) 根据对话中男人的说法，最快到达城镇的方式是乘坐出租车，对话中这个女人说她将听取他的意见，由此可以排除选项（A）坐地铁和（B）坐公交。选项（D）走路去在对话中并没有提及。

41. (B) 单词“reading”在短语“when you have finished reading it”中表明他们正在谈论关于一个书面的文件，这个文件可以是一个报道、一篇新闻或者一本书。（A）副词 yesterday 是指当女人见到杰瑞的时间，不是开会的时间。（C）女人用短语“there’s no rush”来表明她不需要男人立刻返还那本书。“the rush hour”高峰时间是一天中的早上或晚上，当城市由于大批人的上路或者从工作岗位回来造成的拥挤的这段时间。（D）尽管名词“train”在对话中被用到，但没有提到列车时刻表。

42. (C) 办公室从上午9点到下午5:30办公。（A）办公室在工作日办公，不包括周六和周日，（B）它开门办公到下午5:30，不是到下午6:00。（D）说话者解释说办公室 is closed at the moment，意思是它现在没有开门。

43. (B) 西村先生住在东京，他已经在那里生活 20 年了。（A）大阪是他出生的城市，而不是他生活的城市。（C）纽约是他目前所在的城市，而不是永久性的。（D）在对话中没有提到伦敦。

44. (C) 到宾馆走路仅需要10分钟；第二个女人选择走路回她的宾馆，因为她可以很容易地走回那里。（B）第一个女人建议给她叫一辆出租车，但是她没接受。选项（A）“坐公交”或者（D）“坐火车”在对话中都没有被提到。

45. (C) 女人解释说男人两个月以前已经调动或者调转到新的部门。（B）调动到另一个部门并不意味着他不在这家公司工作了。选项（A）“出差”和（D）“在开会”在对话中没有被提到。

46. (A) 男人提到了凯西的婚礼，暗示了她将要结婚。（B）女人应该为凯西的婚礼买一份礼物，而不是为了她的生日或者（C）为了圣诞节。（D）在对话中没有表明浪费了时间。

47. (B) 男人提到了一个航班在 9 点，另一个航班在 11 点，女人选择了第一个，那就是 9 点的航班。（A）男人说有两个航班，而不是在两点钟有一个航班。（C）女人想在 6 月 10 日离开，而不是在 10 点。（D）她没有选择 11 点的航班，因为这是第二个航班。

48. (A) 玛丽莎想告诉男人去 225 房间的路线，这表明她想让他跟着她走。（C）男人向玛丽莎寻求帮助，这暗示他找不到路线，在对话中没有提到（B）“道歉”和（D）“去开会”。

49. (B) “最后一站”和“下车”暗示说话者谈及的是公共交通，这表明男人是一个公交车司机，而不是（D）出租车司机。选项（A）“服务员”和选项（C）“电话接线员”都没有回应去博物馆这个中心意思。

50. (D) 男人解释说乘坐出租车去火车站费用不超过 9 或 10 美元，这意味着车费可能比 9 美元更低，但不会超过 10 美元。这样选项（A）“20 美元”（B）“超过 10 美元”和（C）“8 美元”都被排除。

51. (A) Can 是一个用来请求允许做某事的情态动词，助动词（B）“have”和（D）“had”后面应该跟动词的过去分词。（C）助动词“does”是第三人称单数，因为问题中的主语是第一人称单数，所以不适合用在这里。

52. (C) 只有一般现在时应该用在“as soon as”句型中，而不应使用（A）一般将来时“will”。选项（B）用了现在进行时“am having”和（D）一般过去时“had”都是不适合的。

53. (A) 助动词“did”后面应该跟没有“to”的不定式形式（动词原形），选项（B）“knew”是一般过去时。选项（C）“knowing”是动词的动名词形式。选项（D）“to know”是带“to”的不定式。

54. (A)　在这个句子中，现在完成时形式“have had”是唯一一个表明汽车已经属于我们多久的一个答案。选项（B）“had”用在一般过去时中，选项（C）“have”是一般现在时。选项（D）“are having”是现在进行时。

55. (A)　这个句子中的动词后面应该跟“to”+不定式形式。只有选项（A）“had”是合适的答案。选项（B）“can”,（C）“must not”和（D）“might”后面只能接带 to 的动词不定式。

56. (D)　在短语“Would you mind”之后应该用动词的动名词形式。选项（A）“answered”是过去式或过去分词。选项（B）“to answer”和（C）“answer”都是不定式。

57. (A)　因为“80% of our electronic components（我们 80%的电子零件）”是句子的主语，只有被动语态可以用来描述公司的生产方法。选项（B）“produce”,（C）“are producing”和（D）“produced”都是主动语态。

58. (A)　在这个句子中，“the manager and his staff”作为主语是复数，因此要求动词的复数形式。（B）“meets”是第三人称单数的动词。选项（C）“is meeting”和（D）“are meeting”都是现在进行时，不适合用在这里，因为“once a week”暗示了一个重复的动作，需要用一般现在时形态的动词。

59. (B)　在这个句子中，形容词“responsible”应该与介词“for”一起用，因此排除选项（A）“of”,（C）“from”或（D）“about”。

60. (D)　“at”是唯一正确的用在动词“arrive”后面的介词，后跟地名。介词（A）“of”,（B）“to”和（C）“on”都不能用在这种情况下。

61. (A)　“from”是唯一可以与形容词“different”连用的介词，因此，排除选项（B）“at”,（C）“as”和（D）“of”。

62.　(D)　副词“yet”用在这个问题中来询问是否电子邮件已经被阅读。（A）“last week”是应该与动词一般过去时连用的时间状语。（B）“still”可以用在现在完成时的句子里，但它不应该用在这个位置上。（C）“soon”不能用在现在完成时里。

63.　(C)　副词“hard”表明为了通过考试的方法。（A）“as hard”这个形式通常后接“as”表明一种比较关系。（B）名词“hardship”和（D）副词“hardly 几乎没有”用在这个句子里不合适。

64.　(A)　副词“never”用在这个句子中来表达他根本什么东西也没喝这样一个事实。（B）“ever”通常用在问句中，或是用在含有否定形式动词的句子中。连词（C）“neither”和（D）“either”表示可供选择，所以也不适合用这里。

65.　(B)　代词“anything”应该用在这个问题中来询问是否乘客在他或她的行李中有需要申报的东西。（A）“something”只可以用在肯定句中或者在当我们期望答案是“yes”的问题中。（C）“thin”是一个形容词。在这个句子中，没有需要修饰的名词，因此不能用它。（D）“thing”是一个可数名词，它前面必须有冠词。

66.　(B)　副词“late”与“four hours”连用形成了一个完整的短语，意思是比原计划的时间晚了四小时。（A）“last”可以是形容词，也可以是动词，（C）“latest”是最高级，（D）“lately”是副词，这三个选项都不能表达句子需要的意思。

67.　(D)　副词“fast”描述的是一种危险的驾驶方式，因此排除形容词（A）“quick”和（B）“slow”。（C）“quicker”是形容词比较级，不能放在副词“too”之后。

68.　(D)　名词“bunch”是名词“束”的意思，通常被用来形容捆扎在一起的一样的东西，“a bunch of flowers 一束花”构成了一个完整的短语。名词（A）“piece”，（B）“tin”和（C）“slice”都不能用在这个语境中。

69. (A) 动词“read”用在现在完成时的句子中。动词“to ride”的过去分词形式（B）“ridden”和一般过去时形式（C）“rode”都不能用来指信件。（D）“rid”的意思是“离开”或者“从一个地方丢掉不愉快的东西”，在这种情况下也不适合。

70. (D) 比较级形式“less interesting”是唯一可以用在连词“than”之前的选项。（A）形容词“interesting”不是比较级，所以它不能与“than”连用。（B）表示同级比较的“as interesting”应该与“as”连用，而不是“than”。（C）最高级形式“the most interesting”不能与连词“than”连用。

71. (A) 形容词+“enough”的结构是完成这个句子的唯一方式。（B）在这个句子中，“enough”不能放在形容词“warm”之前。（C）“always”之类的频度副词用来描述重复的动作，而不能描述本句表现的单一的事件。（D）连词“neither”通常与连词“nor”组合在一起，这里不是这种情况。

72. (C) 连词“and”连接两个动名词“reading”和“listening”。按照规则，由连词连接的单词或短语一定有相同的语法结构，因此排除选项（A）“listen”，（B）“to listen”和（D）“listened”。

73. (A) 形容词“foreign”在这个句子中被用来描述马克和希拉里每年都去拜访的国家的类型。（B）“foreigner”是一个名词，不是一个形容词。（C）尽管它和“foreign”意思一样，但“abroad”是副词，不能用在名词前。（D）在这个句子中，介词短语“out of”不能用在名词“country”前。

74. (C) 形容词“thirsty”之前应该是助动词“be”，因此选项（A）“have”，（B）“do”和（D）“will”都不适合。

75. (A) 动词“make”是使役动词，后面通常接宾语+不带“to”的不定式。选项（B）“works”是一般现在时。选项（C）“working”是动名词。选项（D）“worked”要么是过去式，要么是过去分词。

76.　(A)　在这个句子中，动词“keep”后面应该加动名词，表明动作在持续。选项（C）“to make”是不定式形式，在这里是不对的。名词 mistake 不能与出现在选项（B）和（D）中的动词“do”一起使用。

77.　(B)　“must not”表明吸烟是被绝对禁止的。选项（A）“have to”和选项（C）“need to”则表示与之相反的意思。（D）助动词“are”后面从来不会加不定式。

78.　(B)　动词“finished”后面应该加动名词，如“speaking”，其他的选项都不适合。（A）“to speak”和（D）“speak”都是动词的不定式形式，（C）“speaks”是动词的一般现在时形式。

79.　(A)　短语“it is not worth”后面通常跟动名词，所以只有（A）“trying”可以被用在这里。选项（B）“to try”和（C）“try”都不适合，因为都是动词不定式形式。选项（D）“trial”是名词，不是动词。

80.　(B)　由于主句中使用了“would”，在“if”从句中需要用一般过去时。（A）“live”是一般现在时,（C）“living”是动名词，（D）“will live”是一般将来时。

81.　(A)　这个公寓已经被翻新，即装修。（B）广告明确地指出公寓是在六楼，且是有电梯的。（C）公寓里已经有一张床、一个长沙发、一台洗碗机和一台洗衣机，这些表明公寓不是空的。（D）公寓是明亮的，表明光线很好。

82.　(C)　Home Search 是一个代理机构，与之联系就会得到关于公寓的详细信息，因此，它很可能是一个房地产代理机构，而不是（A）旅行社、（B）汽车租赁代理或者（D）广告代理。

83.　(B)　公寓将空出来，即 9 月 30 日可以入住，因此排除（A）这个春季、（C）立刻和（D）在周一。

84.　(C)　广告声称，宠物（像猫或者狗那样可以在房子里养的动物）是不被允许的。这里并没有说（A）儿童、（B）女佣或者（D）

商人不能待在宾馆。

85. (B) 宾馆的规章明确表示，在到达日期前的 24 小时内任何取消或发生变化将要收取 30 美元的费用，这当然包括了在最后一分钟取消预订。但规章并没有说（A）提前结账退房、（C）退款或者（D）使用商务中心要收取额外费用。

86. (A) 礼品，即礼物，可以在宾馆的礼品店买到。（B）尽管健身室被提到，但并没有说也可以预订网球场。（C）30 美元是作为取消预订而收取的费用被提到的，但是没有提到价值 30 美元的书籍。（D）笔记本电脑和手机可以租用（即付钱就可使用），并没有提到汽车可以被租用。

87. (B) （B）该通知提及“客人”，即住在宾馆里的人。因此，宾馆里是最有可能有“客人”的，因此排除选项（A）“在街上”、（C）“在医院里”和（D）“在公交车上”。

88. (D) 因为电梯是直到 9 月 1 日 12:00 才能被修复，所以直到那时电梯才能正常使用。这可以排除选项（A）翻修将会持续下去、（B）翻修阶段将会开始。（C）电梯将被修复，即被修理和改进，但不会被另一部他电梯代替。

89. (C) 由于修复阶段将会在 9 月 1 日结束，这就表明目前这种情况是暂时的。（A）因为是暂时的，所以这种情况不能被看作没有希望的。（B）这种情况可能不会让宾馆的客人和雇员觉得愉快，但是文中没有提到。（D）状况在 9 月将变得更好，即改善。

90. (C) 信息的日期为 3 月 10 日。史蒂文给凯瑞打电话是在 this morning，即在同一天的早上或今天的早些时候。（B）下午 2:30 这个时间和（A）3 月 16 日这个日期都是将举行会议的时间。（D）信息中没有提到昨天早上。

91. (B) 信息中说举行会议是为了讨论新的广告活动。（A）史蒂文为计划的改变而道歉，但没有说将在会议上讨论。（C）展示怎样去到新办公室的地图是这个信息的附件，而不是需要在会议上讨论的事项。（D）没有提到要签署合同。

92.　(A)　史蒂文说已经附加了一个地图来展示怎样去到他公司新的办公室。（B）史蒂文提到了他早上给卡伦打了电话，但是并没有说他希望她给他回电话。（C）史蒂文发送这条信息是为了确认会议，而不是要取消会议或（D）推迟会议。

93.　(D)　文件里说伊桑·阿姆斯特朗很高兴邀请你。因此，他是发出邀请的人。（A）伊桑·阿姆斯特朗是一个人，而不是一群摄影师。选项（B）在文件中没有提到画家。（C）文件里说梅雷迪思·沙利文基金会将获得来自销售的部分收益，并不是邀请函由基金会发出。

94.　(C)　文章表明基金会将会获得部分收益，即收到来自销售的一部分钱。选项（A）“阿姆斯特朗的新书”和（B）“一些照片”在邀请函中没有被提到。（D）基金会将会收到“部分收益”，即收益中的一些，不是全部。

95.　(D)　“他新书里的一部分照片将被出售”暗示了客人可以去购买照片，而不是（A）照片可以免费得到。（B）梅雷迪思·沙利文基金会将得到捐赠，不是伊桑·阿姆斯特朗。（C）没有说招待会上将会拍照片。

96.　(B)　10 月的销售额（售出 12 000 台）和 11 月的销售额（也售出 12 000 台）是相同的。（A）7 月的销售额不比 9 月高，而是恰好相同。（C）销售额在 9 月没有减少反而增加（回到 10 000 台）。（D）销售额在 10 月和 11 月处于相同的水平（12 000 台），但是在 12 月增加到了 14 000 台。

97.　(A)　8 月的销售额下降了，即下跌或减少。但是（B）9 月、（C）10 月和（D）12 月销售额是上升的。

98.　(A)　这些摘录是标题，标题是指总结或者给出一个新闻故事的主题、放在故事的上方和头版、用大号字体印刷的短句子。(B) 文章不是短句而是完整的故事。（C）这些句子不是用疑问的形式。（D）摘要并没有想要做广告，也就是推销商品或事件。

99. (B) 标题“雷德曼联合股价下跌”意思是股票价格在下降，因此排除选项（A）保持在相同的水平。（C）上升和（D）提高都不对，因为这两个词都是“上升”的意思。

100 (A) “总理在行贿丑闻后辞职”意思是政治家因为卷入贿赂丑闻而不得不放弃工作，贿赂是指人们为钱财或礼品做违法的事情。（B）其中一篇文章提到了飓风（猛烈的暴风雨），不是地震（地球表面的突然晃动）。（C）其中一篇文章是关于禁令（官方禁止某事的法令），而不是关于品牌（商标）。（D）其中一篇文章是关于佛罗里达的飓风，不是去那里的旅行。

模拟测试 2 — 听力文本

1.

(A) The people are sitting in a large room.
(B) Several customers are leaving.
(C) The tables are occupied.
(D) A waiter is serving drinks.

（A）人们正坐在一个大房间里。

（B）几名顾客正在离开。

（C）所有桌子都有人了。

（D）服务生正在送饮料。

2.

(A) The man is drawing.
(B) He's hanging a picture on the wall.
(C) He's folding a piece of paper.
(D) He's wearing a cap.

（A）男人正在画画。

（B）他正把画挂到墙上。

（C）他正在折纸。

（D）他正在戴帽子。

3.

(A) The men are feeding the animals.
(B) The dogs are running.
(C) The dogs are resting.
(D) The men are covered in snow.

（A）男人们正在喂动物。

（B）一群狗正在奔跑。

（C）一群狗在休息。

（D）男人们身上全是雪。

4.

(A) It is raining in the park.
(B) The man is running in a park.
(C) The man has fallen on the ground.
(D) He is running out of time.

（A）公园里正在下雨。

（B）男人正在公园里跑步。

（C）男人摔倒在地上。

（D）他没有时间了。

5.

(A) Some cows are standing in the field.
(B) Horses are crossing the field.
(C) The animals are drinking water.
(D) The animals are behind the farm.

（A）一群奶牛正站在田野中。

（B）一群马正穿行在田野中。

（C）动物们正在喝水。

（D）动物们在农场后面。

6.

(A) They are making a fire.
(B) The place is on fire.
(C) A log is burning in the fireplace.
(D) The fire has been put out.

（A）他们正在生火。

（B）那地方着火了。

（C）一根原木正在壁炉里燃烧着。

（D）火已经被熄灭了。

7.

(A) The snow has melted.
(B) There is some snow on the ground.
(C) The houses are covered with snow.
(D) The traffic has been interrupted because of the snow.

（A）雪已经融化了。

（B）地上有一些积雪。

（C）房子上覆盖着雪。

（D）因为大雪，车流被堵塞了。

8.

(A) They are placing the bags into a truck.
(B) The luggage is on the ground.
(C) They are opening the suitcases.
(D) They are inspecting the suitcases.

（A）他们正在把包放进卡车。

（B）行李在地上。

（C）他们正在打开行李。

（D）他们正在检查行李。

9.

(A) The gate is wide open.
(B) There is a car parked in front of the gate.
(C) The gate is made of wood.
(D) There is a sign on the gate.

（A）大门大敞着。

（B）在大门前停着一辆小汽车。

（C）大门是用木头做的。

（D）在大门上有一个标牌。

10.

(A) The motorcycle is running.

(B) The motorcycle is parked.
(C) The man is pushing the motorcycle.
(D) The motorcycle is between a bus and a car.

（A）摩托车正在行驶。

（B）摩托车停放着。

（C）男人正在推摩托车。

（D）摩托车在公共汽车和小汽车之间。

11.
(A) The passengers are getting on the bus.
(B) The bus is empty.
(C) The bus is on the highway.
(D) Some people are leaning against the bus.

（A）乘客们正在上公共汽车。

（B）公共汽车上没有人。

（C）公共汽车行驶在公路上。

（D）一些人正倚靠在公共汽车上。

12.
(A) The man is sailing.
(B) The man is standing near the boat.
(C) The man is sitting in the boat.
(D) The man is pushing the boat into the water.

（A）男人正在航行。

（B）男人正在船边站着。

（C）男人正在船里坐着。

（D）男人正把船推入水中。

13.
(A) The man is sweeping.
(B) The man is weeping.
(C) He is washing the dishes.
(D) He is cooking.

（A）男人正在做扫除。
（B）男人正在哭泣。
（C）他正在刷盘子。
（D）他正在做饭。

14.
(A) They have put up their umbrellas.
(B) The umbrellas are in their cases.
(C) Some children are playing in the street.
(D) They are getting on the bus.

（A）他们已举起他们的雨伞。
（B）雨伞在他们的箱子里。
（C）一些孩子正在街道上玩耍。
（D）他们正在上公共汽车。

15.
(A) The children are wearing caps.
(B) The children are going in the same direction.
(C) They are following a dog.
(D) They are going up the stairs.

（A）孩子们正戴着帽子。
（B）孩子们正向着一个方向走去。
（C）他们正跟随着一条狗。
（D）他们正在上楼梯。

16. (Man 1) How long are you here for?

(Man 2) (A) Less than a week.
(B) It's too long.
(C) I'm here for the conference.

（男 1） 你在这里待多久？

（男 2） （A）不到一个星期。

（B）实在太长时间了。
（C）我来这里是为了参加会议。

17. (Man) Do you agree with me?

(Woman)
(A) Yes, I am.
(B) Not at all.
(C) Next week.

（男）你同意我的意见吗？

（女）
（A）是的，我是。
（B）一点儿也不。
（C）下周。

18. (Woman) You're from Miami, aren't you?

(Man)
(A) That's right.
(B) No, I don't.
(C) I went there by plane.

（女）你来自迈阿密，对吗？

（男）
（A）对。
（B）不，我不。
（C）我坐飞机去的那里。

19 (Woman 1) How long have you worked here?

(Woman 2)
(A) Until Monday.
(B) For two months.
(C) Two months ago.

（女 1）你在这里工作了多久了？

（女 2）
（A）到下周一。
（B）两个月。
（C）两个月前。

20. (Woman) Do you want to visit our showroom?

(Man) (A) There's not enough room.
(B) I'll show you my card.
(C) I've already seen it.

（女） 你想参观我们的展厅吗？

（男） （A）没有足够的空间。
（B）我会给你看我的卡片。
（C）我已经看过了。

21. (Man) Are you free on Thursday?

(Woman) (A) I am busy all day.
(B) Yes, it's free on Thursdays.
(C) I'd like three.

（男） 你周四有空吗？

（女） （A）我一整天都忙。
（B）是的，周四是免费的。
（C）我想要三个。

22. (Woman) How many people do you employ?

(Man) (A) By bus or train.
(B) Five thousand.
(C) In our factory.

（女） 你雇了多少人？

（男） （A）坐公共汽车或者火车。
（B）五千人。
（C）在我们工厂。

23. (Man 1) Where is your head office?

(Man 2) (A) In Europe.
(B) Because he is the manager.
(C) Two years ago.

（男 1）　你们总公司在哪里？

（男 2）　（A）在欧洲。
（B）因为他是经理。
（C）两年前。

24. (Man)　Is this the first time you have been to Chicago?

(Woman)　(A)　It's time to go.
(B)　I've never been here before.
(C)　Yes, I am.

（男）　这是你第一次来芝加哥吗？

（女）　（A）是时候该走了。
（B）我之前从来没来过这里。
（C）是的，我是。

25. (Man)　Are you enjoying your stay?

(Woman)　(A)　Only a few days.
(B)　I'm staying at the hotel.
(C)　Yes, very much.

（男）　你喜欢待在这里吗？

（女）　（A）仅仅几天。
（B）我正在宾馆待着。
（C）是的，非常喜欢。

26. (Man)　Can I get you a coffee?

(Woman)　(A)　Yes, I can.
(B)　Thanks. You too.
(C)　No thanks. I've just had one.

（男）　我给你来杯咖啡怎么样？

（女）　（A）是的，我能。
（B）谢谢，你也一样。

（C）谢谢，不用了，我刚刚喝过一杯。

27. (Man 1)　Is there anything I can do to help?

(Man 2)
(A)　In the office.
(B)　No thanks.
(C)　I can't help it.

（男1）　有什么事我可以帮忙的吗？

（男2）
（A）在办公室。
（B）不用了，谢谢。
（C）我情不自禁。

28. (Woman)　How far is it to the station?

(Man)
(A)　By train.
(B)　2 hours ago.
(C)　2 miles away.

（女）　这里距离车站多远？

（男）
（A）坐火车。
（B）两小时以前。
（C）距离两英里。

29. (Woman)　What's the matter with you?

(Man)
(A)　No, it doesn't matter.
(B)　Nothing. I'm just a bit tired.
(C)　At the office.

（女）　你怎么了？

（男）　（A）不，没关系。
（B）　没事，我只是有点儿累。
（C）　在办公室。

30. (Woman 1) Are you married?

(Woman 2) (A) No, I don't.
(B) He got married last year.
(C) I'm single.

（女 1） 你结婚了吗？

（女 2） （A）不，我不。
（B）他去年结婚了。
（C）我单身。

31. (Man) What are you doing this evening?

(Woman) (A) Nothing special.
(B) I'm afraid I can't.
(C) Every Saturday.

（男） 今晚你要干什么？

（女） （A）没有特别的安排。
（B）我恐怕不行。
（C）每个周六。

32. (Man 1) Are you going to the meeting this afternoon?

(Man 2) (A) I often go there.
(B) Yes, I do.
(C) I'm afraid not.

（男 1） 今天下午你去参加会议吗？

（男 2） （A）我经常去那里。
（B）是的，我是。
（C）我恐怕去不了。

33. (Man 1) Where are you staying in London?

(Man 2) (A) I'm in London for 3 days.
(B) To visit the City.
(C) At the Continental Hotel.

（男 1）　你住在伦敦什么地方？

（男 2）　（A）我在伦敦待三天。

（B）去参观这座城市。

（C）住在洲际酒店。

34. (Man 1) Would you mind opening the window?

(Man 2) (A) It’s very close.

(B) Not at all.

(C) I haven’t made up my mind yet.

（男 1）　您介意我打开窗户吗？

（男 2）　（A）离得很近。

（B）一点儿也不介意。

（C）我还没下定决心。

35. (Woman 1) What exactly does Mr Ashley do?

(Woman 2) (A) He’s gardening.

(B) He’s an engineer.

(C) Because he needs money.

（女 1）　阿什利先生具体是从事什么职业的？

（女 2）　（A）他正在做园艺。

（B）他是一个工程师。

（C）因为他需要钱。

36. (Woman) In Montana and Wyoming, it’ll be mainly dry and sunny. You can expect some rain in the afternoon with temperatures a bit lower than yesterday around 40 or 42 degrees, so rather cold for this time of year.

（女）　在蒙大拿州和怀俄明州，未来天气以干燥和晴朗为主。下午的时候有可能下雨，气温也将比昨天低一些，达到 40～42 度，所以对于一年里的这个时候来说，天气有点儿冷。

37. (Man 1)　So, what's the problem, Mr Murphy?
(Man 2)　I've had a bad stomach ache for the last couple of days. It could be something I ate at the restaurant over the weekend.
(Man 1)　Maybe. I'm going to examine you and give you a prescription.

（男 1）　那么，出现了什么问题，墨菲先生？
（男 2）　这几天我的胃一直非常疼。应该是周末的时候在饭店吃了什么东西。
（男 1）　可能是，我将对你进行检查并给你开药方。

38. (Man)　Good morning, ladies and gentlemen. This is your captain Charles Myers speaking. We are now cruising at an altitude of 30,000 feet. Our arrival time in New York will be delayed by a couple of hours due to bad weather conditions over the Atlantic. I'll give you more details in a few minutes.

（男）　早上好，女士们先生们。我是机长查尔斯·迈尔斯。我们现在正在三万尺的高度飞行。由于大西洋上空恶劣天气条件的影响，我们到达纽约的时间将会延误两个小时。几分钟之后我将会给您带来进一步的信息。

39. (Man)　Good morning. Can I speak to Helen Bates, please?
(Woman)　I'm sorry but her line is engaged. Would you like to leave a message?
(Man)　No, that's all right. I'll try again later.

（男）　早上好，请问我可以和海伦·贝茨通话吗？
（女）　很遗憾她正占线。你愿意留下口信吗？
（男）　不用了，没事。我一会再打过来。

40. (Man)　To cash your traveler's checks, you just need to fill out this form.
(Woman)　Do I have to sign my name on each of the checks?
(Man)　Yes, Madam. Can you also show me your driver's license or passport, please?

（男）　要将你的旅行支票兑换成现金，你仅需要填写这张表格。
（女）　我需要在每一张支票上签名字吗？

（男）　是的，女士。您能给我看一下您的驾照或者护照吗？

41. (Woman) Right after the break, Alex Campbell will join us with the latest business report and then in the last half hour we'll hear an exclusive interview with the world-renowned photographer Malcolm Hudson who has just returned from a 3-year travel experience in Alaska. So stay tuned.

（女）　就在休息之后，亚历克斯·坎贝尔将给我们带来最新的商务报道，在之后的半个小时我们将听到对世界著名摄影师马尔科姆·哈德逊的独家专访，他刚从阿拉斯加旅行 3 年回来。所以别换频道。

42. (Man) I'd like to return this camera and get a refund. Here's the receipt
(Woman) Why do you want to return it?
(Man) It doesn't work.

（男）　我希望退掉这个相机并得到退款。这是发票。
（女）　您为什么想退货呢？
（男）　它不好用。

43. (Woman 1) Can I help you?
(Woman 2) Yes. I'd like to try this swimsuit on. Where's the fitting room?
(Woman 1) It's over there. Near the rest room.

（女 1）　有什么能帮您？
（女 2）　是的，我想试一下这件泳装。试衣间在哪里？
（女 1）　就在那里，洗手间旁边。

44. (Woman) Your attention, please. Passengers traveling to Chicago on flight 269 are requested to proceed to gate number 35. Flight 269 now boarding at gate number 35.

（女）　各位请注意。乘坐 269 号航班去往芝加哥的乘客们需要从 35 号登机口登机。269 号航班现在正在 35 号登机口登机。

45. (Man) Where did you leave the travel brochure about Cyprus?
(Woman) I left it on your desk yesterday.
(Man) I can't find it anywhere.

（男）你把塞浦路斯的旅行手册放在哪儿了？
（女）我昨天放在你的桌子上了。
（男）我哪儿都找不着。

46. (Woman) Good morning, Mr Miller. What can I do for you?
(Man) I'm calling about the office supplies that we ordered last week. When can we expect to get them?
(Woman) Well, I dispatched them yesterday. I guess they'll be delivered tomorrow at the latest.

（女）早上好，米勒先生。我能为您做些什么？
（男）我打电话是想知道我们上周订购的办公用品什么时候能收到？
（女）嗯，我昨天发货了，我想最迟明天你们就能收到了。

47. (Woman) Good morning, Ladies and Gentlemen. Thank you for coming. My name is Patricia Harris and I'm going to give a short presentation on the organization of this company, its sales figures for this year and its strategy for the future. My talk will be very short and if you have any questions to ask, I'll be glad to answer them at the end.

（女）早上好，女士们先生们。感谢你们的到来。我是帕特里夏•哈里斯，我将做一个关于公司的公司结构、今年的销售数据及未来发展战略的报告。我的报告将非常简短，如果你们有什么问题要问，在报告的最后我将会非常高兴为你们解答。

48. (Man) White Valley Restaurant. Can I help you?
(Woman) I'd like to book a table for two for tonight at 8 o'clock.
(Man) I'm afraid we're fully booked until Friday.

（男）这里是白色山谷餐厅，有什么可以帮您的？

（女）　我想预订今晚八点一个两人桌。
（男）　很抱歉，周五前我们预订都满了。

49. (Woman)　Excuse me. Do you know where I can find a post office near here?
(Man)　There's one near Hudson Lane.
(Woman)　Can you tell me how to get there?
(Man)　Sure, Ma'am. It's in the shopping mall, between the travel agency and the department store. You can't miss it.

（女）　打扰了，您知道离这儿最近的邮局在哪儿吗？
（男）　在哈德逊巷附近有一个。
（女）　您能告诉我怎么去能到那儿吗？
（男）　当然可以，女士，它在一个大购物中心里，在旅行社和百货商场之间。您不会找不到的。

50. (Man)　Could you tell me when the business center is open?
(Woman)　It's open between 7:30am and 9:30pm Monday through Friday.
(Man)　Thanks. I'll try to go there this evening.

（男）　您能告诉我商业中心什么时候营业吗？
（女）　周一到周五的上午七点半到晚上九点半营业。
（男）　谢谢，我想办法今晚过去。

模拟测试 2 — 答案

1. (C) 照片中显示人们坐在桌子旁边。（A）人们坐在门外，并不是在屋子里。（B）所有的顾客在坐着，他们没有离开。（D）照片里没有看到服务生。

2. (A) 照片中显示男人在一张纸上画一张脸，因此他的模特一定坐在他的对面。（B）在照片中看不到有墙。（C）男人正在拿着一张纸，没有在折纸。（D）男人光着头，这意味着他头上什么也没戴。

3. (C) 狗儿们正坐在或躺在雪上，这说明它们正在休息。（A）男人正在说话，没有在给动物食物。（B）动物根本没有动。（D）尽管男人在雪地中站着，但他们没有被雪覆盖。

4. (B) 照片中显示男人在奔跑或者慢跑。（A）地上没有湿，这说明没有下雨。（C）没有事实证明男人摔倒在地上。也没有说（D）他在奔跑可能是因为时间紧。

5. (A) 在照片中，我们能看到一群奶牛在田野中。一些在站着，另一些躺在地上。（B）照片中的动物是奶牛，不是马。（C）奶牛并没有在喝任何东西。（D）动物们在田野中，照片中见不到农场。

6. (C) 一根原木，也就是树干的一大段，正在壁炉中燃烧着。（A）火在燃烧着，说明火已经被点着了并且图片中没有人出现。（B）那个地方指的是整个房间，房间也没有着火或者燃烧。（D）可以看到壁炉中的火焰，这说明火没有被熄灭。

7. (B) 在照片中，我们可以看到地上和树上有一些雪，这说明（A）雪还没有融化。图中见不到（C）房子或者（D）车流。

8. (B) 在照片中，我们可以看到地上有一些包和手提箱之类的行李。（A）照片中见不到卡车。没有证据显示人们正在（C）打开或者（D）检查手提箱。

9. (D) 在照片中，我们能看有一个挂有标牌的大门。（A）大门是关着的，不是大敞着的。（B）在大门前见不到小汽车。（C）大门看上去是铁做的，不是木头做的。

10. (B) 照片展现了一辆摩托车沿着人行道停着。因此,（A）它没有在行驶中。（C）没有人在推摩托车。（D）在摩托车前面或后面都没有其他车。

11. (D) 可以看到一些人倚靠在公共汽车上。（A）人们没有在上或者进入公共汽车。（B）由于照片是从远距离拍摄的，所以不可能确定公共汽车上是人满还是空着。（C）公共汽车看起来是停在街道边上的，因此它没有在公路即有好几个车道的大路上。

12. (B) 男人在靠近小船的位置站着。（A）因此，他不可能正在航行或者（C）在船里坐着。（D）男人没有接触小船。因此，他不可能在推船。

13. (A) 照片显示一个男人正在用扫帚清扫地板。（B）没有证据显示他正在哭泣或者流眼泪。（C）男人正在清扫地板，没有在刷盘子或者（D）在做饭。

14. (A) 照片中人们正在用雨伞挡雨。（B）因为雨伞正被用着，所以伞不可能在他们的箱子里。（C）在照片中见不到孩子。（D）尽管我们能看到在举着雨伞的人们前面有公共汽车路过，但看不出来他们正在上公共汽车。

15. (B) 孩子们看起来是在一起的。在图片中他们是向着一个方向也就是向左走的。（A）三个孩子光着头，他们没有戴帽子。（C）图片中没有狗出现，并且（D）也没有楼梯。

16. (A) 在这个问题中，关键词是“how long”，所以一段时间是正确答案。选项（B）重复问题中的单词“long”，但是意思不同。

（C）是回答“why”的问题。

17.　(B)　男人想要知道女人是否和他的观点一致。她表明她完全不同意男人的观点。（A）单词 am 不能用来回答用 do 来提问的问题。选项（C）回答的是“when”的问题。

18.　(A)　女人想要知道男人是否真的来自迈阿密。他确认他是来自迈阿密。（B）don’t 不能用来回答以 be 提问的是非问题。选项（C）回答交通方式的问题，并不是男人来自的地方。

19.　(B)　这里关键的疑问词是 how long，后面是现在完成时，所以答案应该包括一段到现在为止的时间。选项（A）中有表示结束的时间点，时间点并不能与现在完成时连用。选项（C）指的是过去。

20.　(C)　女人想要知道男人是否有兴趣参观展厅。男人解释说他已经看过了，暗示说他没有兴趣再看一遍了。选项（A）和（B）重复单词 room 和 show，但是和问题中的词义不同。

21.　(A)　男人问女人周四是否有空。她解释说她一整天都忙，暗示她周四没空。选项（B）重复问题中的单词 free，但是词义不同。选项（C）混淆了发音相似的词 three 和 free。

22.　(B)　这里关键的疑问词是 how many，所以数字是正确答案。选项（A）回答关于“how”的问题，不是“how many”的问题。选项（C）回答关于地点的问题。

23.　(A)　关键词是 where，所以地点是正确答案。选项（B）回答“why”的问题。选项（C）回答“when”的问题。

24.　(B)　男人想要知道女人以前是否来过芝加哥。她解释说她没有来过。选项（A）重复问题中的单词 time，但是词义不同。（C）与“the first time”相对应的主格代词应该是“it”不是“I”。

25.　(C)　男人想要知道女人这一天是否愉快。她回答她很愉快。选项（A）回答她准备待多久的问题。选项（B），她说她待在什么地方，并没说她是否喜欢待在那里。

26. (C) 男人要给女人拿一杯咖啡。女人拒绝了，因为她刚刚喝过一杯咖啡。选项（A）重复问题中的主语，不适合回答以 Can I 开头的表示提供帮助的问题。（B）不适合回复提供帮助的请求。

27. (B) 第一个男人要给第二个提供帮助，第二个男人拒绝了好意。选项（A）回答关于地点的问题。选项（C）重复问题中的单词 can 和 help，但是词义不同。

28. (C) 关键词是 how far，所以一段距离是正确答案。选项（A）回答“how”的问题，而不是“how far 距离多远”。选项（B）指的是在过去的一段时间。

29. (B) 女人想要知道男人出了什么问题。他解释说他只是有点儿累。选项（A）重复问题中的单词“matter”，但是词义不同。选项（C）回答了“where”的问题，并不是“what's the matter 发生了什么”的问题。

30. (C) 第一个女人想知道第二个女人是否已婚。第二个女人解释说她是单身，就是说没有结婚。（A）助动词 don't 不能用来回答以 are 提问的问题。（B）主格代词 he 不能指代两位谈话者中的任何一个。

31. (A) 在这个问题中，关键疑问词 what 指的是今天晚上的计划。女人没有计划任何事情。选项（B）只能用来拒绝邀请。选项（C）回答“when”或者“how often”的问题。

32. (C) 第二个男人表明他不会参加会议。选项（A）是一个关于第二个男人通常所做的事情的一般现在时的句子，不是关于他下午将要做什么事情。（B）助动词 do 不能用来回答以 are 提问的问题。

33. (C) 关键词是 where，所以地址是正确答案。选项（A）回答“how long 多远”的问题。选项（B）回答问题“why”。

34. (B) “would you mind”表示请求允许。第二个男人表明他同意打开窗户，即他不反对打开窗户。选项（A）close 是形容词，不是动词。选项（C）重复问题中的单词 mind，但是词义不同。

35. (B) 问题是关于阿什利先生的职业。他是一名工程师。（A）gardening（做园艺）是一个动词，不是工作名称。选项（C）回答关于“why”的问题。

36. (B) 广播员说气温将比昨天低一些，暗示将比昨天冷一些。（A）她解释说天气将会干燥，即不潮湿，并没有提到单词 windy（多风）。（C）天气预报提到下午有雨，并不是一整天都下雨。（D）根本没有提到可能会下雪。

37. (A) 谈话者提到单词肚子疼 stomach ache，检查 examine 和开药方 prescription。这些单词表明谈话发生在医生的诊所里，并不是（B）在商店里。（C）第一个男人（医生）将会检查第二个男人（患者）并且给他开药方；因此他不会是在药房。（D）第二个男人提到他胃疼可能是周末在餐馆里吃了什么东西造成的，说明现在他不在餐馆中。

38. (C) 迈尔斯机长提到班机将会延误两个小时，也就是说航班将会晚点两个小时。（A）换句话说，班机将不会准时到达。（B）他通知乘客将会在几分钟之后发布更多的消息，而不是说航班将会在几分钟之后到达。选项（D）没有在对话中提到。

39. (B) 男人不能和贝茨女士通电话，因为她的电话占线或者正忙。（A）女人请他留下口信，但是他不想。女士解释说电话占线，也就是说（C）他没有拨错号码，并且（D）贝茨女士在办公室里，并没有在外地。

40. (A) 男人向女人解释，可以用什么方式去兑现她的旅行支票。将支票兑现意思是将它换成现金。这说明她是想要一些现金，而不是（B）用支票付款。男人提到（C）驾照和（D）护照是作为身份证明去将支票兑换成现金，但并没有说她把驾照弄丢了或者她需要一个新护照。

41. (A) 亚历克斯·坎贝尔是一名记者，他将会在休息之后带来最新的商务报道。（B）他不是一名摄影师同，而是在休息之后将会接受采访的嘉宾。选项（C）和（D）重复通告中的单词 travel 和 business，但并不是指他的职业。

42. (A) 退款是指还款的数额。这意味着男人想要回他的钱。他并不想（B）买或者（C）卖相机，而是想退还有问题的相机。选项（D）重复对话中的动词 return。

43. (B) 对话者提到词组 try on 和 fitting room，两个都和商场有关。选项（A）混淆了近音词 swimsuit 和 swimming pool。泳衣是衣服的名称，并不是地点。选项（C）在对话中没有提到银行。选项（D）没有提到餐馆，只是提到了休息室或者洗手间。

44. (D) 通告中提到的单词 passengers，flight，boarding 都和机场有关。因此这篇通告不可能（A）在餐馆、（B）在医院或者（C）在公共汽车站听到。

45. (A) 男人提到他到处找不到旅行手册，尽管女人前一天把它放在男人的桌子上了，说明他把手册弄丢了。选项（B）混淆了近音动词 leave 和 live，但是没有说明男人住在塞浦路斯。选项（C）重复对话中的动词 left。（D）宾格代词 it 指代旅行手册，不是桌子。

46. (D) 米勒先生打电话想要知道他订购的办公室用品为什么还没收到。（A）男人提到用品此前一周就订购了。（B）因为米勒先生是顾客，所以送货不是他的工作。（C）没有提到米勒先生想取消订单。

47. (D) 说话者将会做一个简短的发言，即一个简明的谈话。（A）她解释说发言有一部分是关于销售数据，不是关于生产数据。（B）在谈话的最后她邀请观众提问题，但是没说她会问任何问题。（C）发言关于公司结构、销售和战略，不是关于新产品。

48. (A) 女人想要预约或者预订一桌。（B）在对话中，book 是动词，意思是预订，不是名词。（C）女人不能取消她的预订，因为她没有预订过。（D）女人想要在今晚预订一桌，并不是在周五。

49. (D) 男人解释说邮局是在购物中心里。它不是（A）在旅行社或者（B）百货商场，而是在二者之间。（C）邮局不在哈德森巷，而是靠近哈德森巷。

50. (D) 商务中心是上午 7:30 到晚上 9:30 营业，说明在晚上 9:40 已经下班了。女人说商务中心周一到周五营业。因此（A）在周四和（B）周五正常营业。（C）7:30 是营业时间，不是下班时间。

51. (B) 动词 expect 通常后跟宾语+ to +不定式。选项（A）arrive 是不带 to 的不定式。选项（C）arriving 是动名词。选项（D）arrived 是动词过去式或者过去分词形式。

52. (C) 这句话是一般疑问句，因此应该由助动词开头，后面跟主语和动词。（A）没有助动词 do。（B）have 在这里是表示状态的动词，即动词描述的是状态而不是一个动作，所以它不能用于进行式。（D）没有动词。

53. (A) 这里要求过去式 went，表示过去特定时间发生的事情。选项（B）have gone 和选项（C）have been 是现在完成时。选项（D）go 是一般现在时。

54. (B) 句子中应该包含一个动词，后跟带 to 的不定式。只有选项（B）have 是合适的答案。选项（A）must，（C）should 和（D）will 后面只能接不带 to 的不定式。

55. (B) 动词 agreed 应该后跟 to + 动词不定式。选项（A）buy 是不带 to 的不定式。选项（C）buying 是动名词。选项（D）buyer 是名词，不是动词。

56.　(A)　在这句话中，动词 think 是表示状态的动词，表示一个个人观点；（B）因此它不能用于进行时。选项（C）thinks 和（D）thinking 是错误的，因为它们都没有主语。

57.　(C)　复数名词 some people 应该跟随第三人称复数动词。选项（A）likes 是第三人称单数。选项（B）like to 应该接动词不定式，而不是动名词。（D）some people 是动词 like 的主语。只需要一个主语，因此代词 they 在这个句中没必要。

58.　(A)　of 是唯一可以与 in charge 构成完整表达的介词，因此排除选项（B）for,（C）with 和（D）to。

59.　(B)　to 是可以与 right way+动词不定式连用的正确介词。（A）当下一个动词是动名词时，词组 right way 可以接介词 of。选项（C）for 和（D）through 不能用来使该句完整。

60.　(B)　from 是和 different 搭配的正确的介词，排除了选项（A）of。（C）短语 same as 前面常有定冠词 "the"。（D）词组 the same 后常跟随 "as"。

61.　(A)　介词 during 应该用在句中去指代过去的一段时间。（B）when 通常被用作疑问词或者引导一个包含动词的从句。（C）while 和（D）as soon as 不能用在此处，因为它们经常后接带动词的从句。

62.　(C)　最高级 cheapest 应该被用在句中。（A）cheaply 是副词，不能接名词。形容词比较级（B）cheaper 和（D）less cheap 用在这里不合适。

63.　(D)　这里应该使用副词 yet，用来表示火车仍然停在车站。（A）never 不能和动词的否定形式连用。（B）still 和（C）always 用在这里是不对的。

64.　(B)　make 是唯一可以与 mistakes 连用构成完整短语的动词，排除动词（A）do,（C）take 和（D）speak。

65. (A) advised 是四个选项中唯一可以用来接人称代词 him 的，排除选项（B）suggested,（C）said 和（D）explained。

66. (D) talk 是唯一可以在后面接介词 to+宾语的选项，排除选项（A）phone,（B）tell 和（C）call。

67. (C) 连词 as 是唯一可以跟在 the same 之后的选项，表示同级比较，排除（A）than,（B）that 和（D）like。

68. (A) 这里使用副词 too 表明她最好的朋友也被邀请了。（B）尽管 also 和 too 有同样的意思，但是 also 不能用在句末。（C）在这个位置，连词 either 通常用在否定句中。（D）both 作为代词不应该用在这个位置。

69. (D) 频率副词 always 总是应该放在动词 work 之前，组成完整的句子。表达频率的短语像（A）every week 和（B）once a week 不是频率副词，因此它们不能放在动词 work 之前。（C）as well 不能用在问题中的这个位置。

70. (A) 连词 neither 通常和连词 nor 成对使用，但是不能和（B）didn't receive，即动词的否定形式一起使用。（C）neither 不能和连词 and 成对使用。（D）neither 不能和连词 either 成对使用。

71. (A) 这里应该使用一般过去时去表示发生在过去某个时间段的事情，即六个月之前。选项（B）am joining 是现在进行时。选项（C）join 和（D）joins 是一般现在时。

72. (B) 动词 let 应该后接宾语+不带 to 的不定式。（A）let 不能接带 to 的不定式。（C）动名词 watching 和（D）一般现在时 that she watches 不能用在 let 之后。

73. (A) 在上下文中，动词 made 经常接宾语+不带 to 的不定式。选项（B）to laugh 不是不带 to 的不定式。选项（C）laughing 是动名词。选项（D）laughter 不是动词，而是名词。

74. (A) 在这个句子中，动词 asked 应该和介词 for 连用，因为后接一个名词（directions）。（B）它后面不能用 to，因为 to 后面要接动词。动词 ask 是不可能后接（C）of 或者（D）at。

75. (A) 短语 thank you 应该后接介词 for，排除选项（B）of,（C）with 和（D）about。

76. (C) on 是介词，在一周的某一天前用，像这里的 Monday。（A）June 是一个月份，前面应该是“in”，而不是 on。（B）形容词 next 和（D）副词 tomorrow 前面不能使用介词 on。

77. (D) with 是唯一正确的介词，可以使句子 he's not very pleased 完整，因此排除选项（A）of,（B）to 和（C）at。

78. (A) 介词 until 意思是“在一个特定的时间之前”，应该用在这个句子中。（B）as soon as 和（C）while 通常接动词。（D）yet 不能接名词。

79. (B) 在这个句子中，应该使用连词 and 来连接两个名字 Sam 和 Rachel。连词（A）or 和（C）either 表示可以选择，不适合与 both 连用。（D）连词 but 不能用于连接两个放在 both 后的名字。

80. (A) made 是唯一可以使句子 a lot of progress 完整的动词，排除（B）done,（C）taken 和（D）been。

81. (C) 便条的目的是解释贾斯汀如何从车站去梅根的新房子。（A）梅根说她很高兴贾斯汀能来她的生日派对，说明贾斯汀被邀请了。（B）根据她写的，梅根已经搬进新房了里了；她不会去再买一个房子了。（D）这一点在文章中没有提到。

82. (A) 梅根解释说她的新房子坐落在公共图书馆的旁边，即接近或靠近这个建筑。（B）没有说明梅根的新房子坐落在书店附近。（C）梅根住在 River Road 和 Oakridge Street 的拐角，但是不意味着她的房子在河对面。（D）尽管文章中提到 Lincoln Street，但是梅根的房子不在那里。

83.　(A)　梅根告诉贾斯汀“走出车站”并在“第一条街道右转”即出车站右转。（B）他应该路过 Memorial Church，即沿着教堂一直走，而不是穿过教堂。（C）梅根的弟弟可能在车站接贾斯汀，不是贾斯汀在车站接梅根的弟弟。（D）贾斯汀应该过桥，即在桥上走过它，而不是走到桥下面。

84.　(D)　这篇文章的写作目的是告知乘客，长距离乘坐飞机旅行可能会让人感觉紧张，而且因为生物钟的原因可能会感到困扰。（A）尽管矿泉水被提及，但是不是文章的目的。（B）文章中没有说机票打折。（C）尽管单词 flight 被提及，但是文章的目的不是取消航班。

85.　(C)　出发前睡个好觉是五个提示中的一个。它意思是建议大家起飞前的那晚要好好睡觉。文章建议喝矿泉水来代替（A）喝咖啡或者（B）喝茶。（D）文章中没有提到穿什么样式的衣服。

86.　(C)　在飞行前或飞行时尽量做锻炼，即为了保持健康做身体运动，是帮助释放压力的五条建议之一。（A）文章解释说，提前计划旅行比到最后一刻才计划要好。（B）文章是关于坐飞机旅行，不是关于坐船。（D）没有说明经常旅行是危险的。

87.　(A)　*Science Today* 是一个季度节目，即每年播放四次或者每三个月播放一次。（B）*Newsline business Update* 是日播节目，即每天都能看到。（C）*Insights 2000* 每周能看两次。（D）*Eye on Hi-Tech* 是每周五播放一次。

88.　(B)　*Insights 2000* 是关于政治形势和问题的，排除选项（A）运动、（C）商业和（D）环境。

89.　(C)　*Eye on Hi-Tech* 是每周五播放一次，排除选项（A）每天、（B）每两周和（D）一周两次。

90.　(D)　诺曼・瓦茨是一个小说家或者作者。他写小说，即有关虚构的人物或者故事。虽然文章提到了大学新闻奖，但是诺曼・瓦茨既不是（A）学生，也不是（B）教授。（C）文章没有说诺曼·瓦茨是一名记者。

91. (A) 诺曼·瓦茨将会在都市中心讨论他的新书，说明这将会是一个文学讨论。（B）虽然提到地点是新的都市中心，但是通知并不是关于中心开业的。尽管诺曼·瓦茨是获奖者，但是没有提到会有（C）颁奖礼，或者（D）鸡尾酒派对。

92. (B) 想要知道关于这个活动更多信息的人，可以拨打通告中的电话号码，但是没有说要订票。（A）这个活动将在 5:30 到 7:30 举行，即将会持续两个小时。（C）作家将会介绍他的新小说，说明他将会谈到他的新书 *Murder at the Opera*。（D）通告中说诺曼·瓦茨是一名著名的小说家，说明他因为他的文学天赋而出名和被认可。

93. (A) Orion SL-300i 是数字或电子记事本。（B）句子 Say good bye to your paper organizers 说明 Orion SL-300i 要取代旧式纸质记事本。（C）虽然 Orion SL-300i 允许用户存储照片，但是没有说明它有照相机功能，能用来拍照。（D）Orion SL-300i 不是台式电脑，但是可以和台式电脑共享信息。

94. (C) 就像在广告的最后对用户承诺的，内存卡允许用户扩展或者增加 Orion SL-300i 电子记事本的存储能力。（A）文本中没有提到会有折扣。（B）虽然单词 expensive 和 expansion 在拼写上近似，但是它们的意思不同：expensive 是形容词，意思是“昂贵的”，而 expansion 是名词，意思是“成长”和“发展”。因为内存卡是免费获得的，所以不能说是昂贵的。（D）虽然在广告中用了单词 alarms，但是没有明确说明如果顾客现在购买 Orion SL-300i 就可以得到一个闹钟。

95. (D) 广告说 Orion SL-300i 可以和台式电脑共享信息。换句话说，它可以和电脑交换数据。选项（A）、（B）和（C）在广告中没有被提及。

96. (B) 图表为我们提供了一组数据，数据是关于在最近三年来，我们最经常看的电视节目类型，不是（A）明年。（C）文章中没有提到为儿童设计的节目。（D）没有提供每座城市的详细数据。

97.　(B)　音乐节目仅仅占 5%，是最不常看的电视节目类型。（A）地方和国内新闻占 15% 和（C）体育新闻占 26% 都是比音乐节目更常看的节目。（D）电影占 44%，是最常看的电视节目类型。

98.　(A)　旅行被安排在 6 月 10 日周四，是在第二周而不是在第三周，虽然文章提及关于这次旅行的报告要在第三周进行打印。（B）这次报告计划在 16 日周三进行，即在第三周。（C）牙医的预约是一种医疗预约，并且（D）西班牙语课程是语言课程，两个都安排在第三周。

99.　(B)　这份报告将在 17 日周四上午 10 点被打印出来，即早上 10 点整。这个月周四早上不会安排其他活动。缩写 pm 是“在下午”的意思，所以（A）去波士顿的旅行，（C）培训课程和（D）电台采访都是不正确的。

100.　(D)　在日历里，周六仅安排了三个活动。婚宴是一个典礼或者对结婚的一种祝贺，这说明迪伦和艾米在 19 日周六结婚。（A）在 26 日周六提到的生日礼物是给泰瑞的，所以不是泰瑞买的。（B）在 26 日周六提到单词 present（礼物），但是与 presentation（演讲）没有任何关系。（C）没有说周六会有人搬去新房子里。

附录 C

不规则动词表

不规则动词表

（括号中是替代的英式拼写）

	原形	过去式	过去分词
A	to awake	awoke	awoken
B	to be	was/were	been
	to bear	bore	borne
	to beat	beat	beaten
	to become	became	become
	to begin	began	begun
	to bend	bent	bent
	to bet	betted (bet)	betted (bet)
	to bind	bound	bound
	to bite	bit	bitten
	to blow	blew	blown
	to break	broke	broken
	to breed	bred	bred
	to bring	brought	brought
	to build	built	built
	to burn	burned (burnt)	burned (burnt)
	to buy	bought	bought
C	to catch	caught	caught
	to choose	chose	chosen
	to come	came	come
	to cost	cost	cost
	to creep	crept	crept
	to cut	cut	cut
D	to deal	dealt	dealt
	to dig	dug	dug
	to do	did	done
	to draw	drew	drawn
	to dream	dreamed (dreamt)	dreamed (dreamt)
	to drink	drank	drunk
	to drive	drove	driven
E	to eat	ate	eaten

	原形	过去式	过去分词
F	to fall	fell	fallen
	to feed	fed	fed
	to feel	felt	felt
	to fight	fought	fought
	to find	found	found
	to fly	flew	flown
	to forbid	forbade	forbidden
	to forget	forgot	forgotten
	to forgive	forgave	forgiven
G	to get	got	got
	to give	gave	given
	to go	went	gone
	to grow	grew	grown
H	to hang	hung	hung
	to have	had	had
	to hide	hid	hidden
	to hit	hit	hit
	to hold	held	held
	to hurt	hurt	hurt
K	to keep	kept	kept
	to know	knew	known
L	to lay	laid	laid
	to lead	led	led
	to lean	leaned (leant)	leaned (leant)
	to learn	learnt	learnt
	to leave	left	left
	to lend	lent	lent
	to let	let	let
	to lie	lay	lain
	to light	lit	lit
	to lose	lost	lost

	原形	过去式	过去分词
M	to make	made	made
	to mean	meant	meant
	to meet	met	met
P	to pay	paid	paid
	to put	put	put
Q	to quit	quit	quit
R	to read	read	read
	to ride	rode	ridden
	to ring	rang	rung
	to rise	rose	risen
	to run	ran	run
S	to say	said	said
	to see	saw	seen
	to seek	sought	sought
	to sell	sold	sold
	to send	sent	sent
	to set	set	set
	to shake	shook	shaken
	to shed	shed	shed
	to shine	shone	shone
	to shoot	shot	shot
	to show	showed	shown
	to shut	shut	shut
	to sing	sang	sung
	to sink	sank	sunk
	to sit	sat	sat
	to sleep	slept	slept
	to smell	smelled (smelt)	smelled (smelt)
	to sow	sowed	sowed (sown)
	to speak	spoke	spoken
	to spell	spelled (spelt)	spelled (spelt)
	to spend	spent	spent
	to spill	spilled (spilt)	spilled (spilt)
	to spit	spat	spat
	to split	split	split
	to spoil	spoiled (spoilt)	spoiled (spoilt)
	to spread	spread	spread
	to spring	sprang	sprung
	to stand	stood	stood
	to steal	stole	stolen
	to stick	stuck	stuck
	to sting	stung	stung
	to stride	strode	stridden
	to strike	struck	struck
	to strive	strove	striven
	to sweep	swept	swept
	to swell	swelled	swelled (swollen)
	to swim	swam	swum
T	to take	took	taken
	to teach	taught	taught
	to tear	tore	torn
	to tell	told	told
	to think	thought	thought
	to throw	threw	thrown
U	to understand	understood	understood
W	to wake	woke	woken
	to wear	wore	worn
	to weave	weaved (wove)	weaved (woven)
	to wet	wetted (wet)	wetted (wet)
	to win	won	won
	to write	wrote	written

Achieve TOEIC Bridge™: Test-Preparation Guide, 1e
Renald Rilcy

Cengage Learning Asia Pte. Ltd.
151 Lorong Chuan, #02-08 New Tech Park, Singapore 556741

北京市版权局著作权合同登记号 01-2015-6538

图书在版编目（CIP）数据

托业桥考试全攻略/（美）罗纳德·赖利（Renald Rilcy）编著；蒋璀玢译. —北京：中国人民大学出版社，2017.3

ISBN 978-7-300-23799-2

Ⅰ.①托… Ⅱ.①罗…②蒋… Ⅲ.①英语水平考试-自学参考资料 Ⅳ.①H310.41

中国版本图书馆 CIP 数据核字（2016）第 312497 号

托业桥考试全攻略

［美］罗纳德·赖利（Renald Rilcy） 编著

蒋璀玢　译

Tuoyeqiao Kaoshi Quangonglüe

出版发行	中国人民大学出版社		
社　　址	北京中关村大街 31 号	**邮政编码**	100080
电　　话	010-62511242（总编室）		010-62511770（质管部）
	010-82501766（邮购部）		010-62514148（门市部）
	010-62515195（发行公司）		010-62515275（盗版举报）
网　　址	http://www.crup.com.cn		
	http://www.lkao.com.cn（中国 1 考网）		
经　　销	新华书店		
印　　刷	北京鑫丰华彩印有限公司		
规　　格	185mm×260mm 16 开本	**版　　次**	2017 年 3 月第 1 版
印　　张	22	**印　　次**	2017 年 3 月第 1 次印刷
字　　数	315 000	**定　　价**	39.80 元